Screenwriting

3 Manuscripts in 1 Book, Including: How to Write a Screenplay, How to Tell a Story and How to Edit Writing

Jaiden Pemton

More by Jaiden Pemton

Discover all books from the Creative Writing Series by Jaiden Pemton at:

bit.ly/jaiden-pemton

Book 1: *How to Write Fiction*

Book 2: *How to Tell a Story*

Book 3: *How to Write a Screenplay*

Book 4: *How to Write Sales Copy*

Book 5: *How to Edit Writing*

Book 6: *How to Self-Publish*

Book 7: *How to Write Non-Fiction*

Book 8: *How to Write Content*

Themed book bundles available at discounted prices:

bit.ly/jaiden-pemton

Copyright

Table of Contents

Book 1: How to Write a Screenplay

7 Easy Steps to Master Screenwriting, Scriptwriting, Writing a Movie & Television Writing

Jaiden Pemton

Introduction

There are thousands of ideas for screenplays floating around in such a booming industry, and directors, producers, managers, and executives don't have time to get through them all. The industry is cutthroat, and therefore it is crucial to develop screenwriting skills that set you apart and get your screenplays into the hands of the right people.

It can be easy to find yourself writing screenplays that are too much like what already exists when it comes to screenwriting. You may struggle to get producers to read past your logline, and even if they do, you may find that engagement is lost before the play has come through to the end. It is easy to fall into the trap of using clichés, creating boring dialogues, or being too predictable in the unfolding of events. When it comes to screenwriting, there are several elements to keep in mind to ensure that your audience is engaged and that your story will live on with them and distinguish you in the industry for years to come.

Screenwriting can seem like a daunting task, especially in today's age, where thousands of people are trying to make it in this industry. That being said, all screenwriters still hope to discover the elements of their experience that set them apart and can be tapped into to create one-of-a-kind screenplays. All it takes is an in-depth knowledge of screenwriting aspects that will make producers, managers, and audience members alike care about what is being told to them and want to stick around for the shining moment.

This guide will serve as your step-by-step reference through the realm of screenwriting—breaking down the details within each step of the process and helping you to understand what makes legendary screenplays.

The chapters of this guide will take you through each step of screenwriting in a way that will help you check all the boxes and avoid common mistakes. Together, we will explore the best techniques for catching attention, developing characters, developing plot, creating dialogue, writing first drafts, conducting revisions, getting started, and staying on track. Each detail is designed to keep you on track and answer any questions you may have about the screenwriting process.

Each chapter is organized in an easy-to-follow, subtitled format with comprehensive examples of every tip, trick, and technique. This all-inclusive guide to screenwriting also contains a few exclusive secrets and information that can further develop your skills and create impactful screenplays. No matter what sorts of scripts you aim to write and who you are trying to appeal to, this guide has all the tools you need and is sure to serve as the perfect guide to revolutionize your storytelling experience.

Happy writing!

Chapter 1: Step 1 - Developing your Logline

Like most writing pieces, you must know what kind of story you wish to tell before beginning your screenwriting process. When it comes to screenwriting, the phrase that answers the question: "What is this about?" is called a logline. Traditionally, loglines have been printed on screenplays' spines to allow producers to get an idea of what a screenplay would be about. The logline was ultimately what helped producers to decide if reading the script was worth their time. Today, while the logline is not always printed on a screenplay's spine, it serves the same purpose through verbal communication or along with a treatment (which we will discuss in a later section).

The logline is used to summarize the story, typically in a single sentence, and it strives to convey the thesis, tone, and emotions of your story. The standard word count for a logline is about 30 words, but some cases are exceptions (some complicated screenplays need a logline that is several sentences).

Setting the Precedent

Your logline should provide some insight into what happens in the story and the style in which it will unfold, and how the audience should expect to feel. Within the logline, you will also set a precedent for both your protagonist (the hero/main character) and your antagonist (villain/rival). There are four essential elements to a solid logline, which are as follows: Introduce the protagonist, the incident that triggers a reaction, the goal of the protagonist as they deal with the experience, and the central conflict the character faces. Regardless of which order these things are mentioned in, it is vital to ensure that your logline addresses all four elements.

Identifying the Protagonist

When you identify the protagonist, it is crucial to include detailed descriptions of their physical attributes, personality, and life story. After you have mapped this out, choose an adjective and proper noun combination that accurately describes them. If you are writing a screenplay about a poet named Annie from New York who spends her days working in a bakery and takes the subway to the same hole-in-the-wall speakeasy to perform her work and learn from other poets, you may describe her as a "fervent poet."

Inciting Incident/Triggering Action

The next step after identifying the protagonist is to describe the incident, which triggers a reaction. This is the catalyst for your screenplay; it is the event that gets things going. What is the thing that comes into your character's life and completely changes everything? This incident can be either positive or negative; whichever you choose, make sure it is drastic.

In the case of the poet, let's imagine a positive triggering incident. Let's imagine that one night at the speakeasy, a well-established poet from Atlanta called Blaire stumbles in and is so wowed by what she hears from Annie that she asks to take her on as an apprentice and help her publish her first collection. For the logline, this event needs to be summarized in several words, such as: "when she receives the offer of a lifetime from a well-established poet from Atlanta."

Defining the Protagonist's Goal

Another crucial element of the logline is the protagonist's goal. Whatever that goal is, it will serve as the force around which all other activities in the story revolves. This can be expressed in the logline by describing to the reader what it is that the protagonist needs or wants. Annie's goal, for example, is to be a successful poet. That is what she wants; it is the reason she works a day job at a bakery and takes the subway across the city to a hole-in-the-wall speakeasy even on her most tired days, gets home late at night to eat a microwave dinner and write a few lines before bed, and ultimately, take the opportunity to move to Atlanta for the opportunities she sees for herself to be an apprentice and become published.

Creating a Central Conflict

The final element for drafting a successful logline is to present a central conflict that inflicts a sense of excitement and emotion. What possible obstacles may keep your protagonist from achieving their goal? These obstacles can be people, relationships, physical, psychological, or emotional challenges, etc. Is Annie going to face conflict because she misses New York and is flooded with challenges in Atlanta? Will she struggle because she catches feelings for Blaire and no longer knows how to maintain a healthy work relationship? Does she have to leave Atlanta because of it? Or perhaps, she and Blaire kindle a relationship which directly impacts Annie's success, especially as Blaire becomes abusive and controlling of her, and she feels trapped in a city far away from any support system.

Brainstorm several possible conflicts, select the one that is most high stakes, and summarize it using only a few words. An example of this would be "a perilous romance." The following serves as an example of a logline for Annie's story: "When a fervent poet from New York gains the unexpected opportunity for her next big break, she moves to a new city, only to be swept up in a perilous romance that could either make or break her career."

Gaining Visibility and Holding Attention

Screenwriting is incredibly competitive, and as such, there is no time to wait to grab producers' attention. Because the logline is often the first thing a producer looks at, crafting a great one could be the difference between you and thousands of other aspiring screenwriters. For most screenplay competitions, film festivals, and further showcase opportunities, it is the logline that determines whether your screenplay will become accepted.

Therefore, the logline is one of the most important aspects of becoming accepted to opportunities to gain visibility as a screenwriter and get your work out there to producers and executives. Producers, managers, and agents are flooded with script ideas and do not have time to dig into each one's details. This is why a good logline is so important—it is the thing that may catch their attention long enough to implore them to read your script.

Summarizing your Pitch

Another benefit of writing a good logline is how it can help you summarize your pitch, that is, the way you will present your screenplay idea to other people. The more engaging your logline, the more attractive your pitch will be. The confidence and concise nature with which you describe your screenplay is crucial to capturing and keeping the audience's attention.

Master Tips for Crafting your Logline

Use action words to describe what happens. Make sure the language you choose can be easily transferred to actions on stage or screen. Be unconventional. Make it clear from the very beginning that what happens in this story is something the reader will not be able to predict—compel them to come on the journey of this screenplay, and let them know they are in for a wild ride.

Hook your reader with a dramatic narrative. Draw them in but do not give away the ending-- leave them on the edge of their seats, with no choice but to read the rest of the script.

Chapter 2: Step 2 - Bringing the Screenplay to Life Through Character Development

When it comes to bringing a screenplay to life, it must have fully developed and wide-ranging characters. As human beings, we all have different life experiences, passions, speaking styles, and general presence in the world. All of these are things that must be taken into careful account when it comes to character development. When developing characters in screenwriting, you must consider the physical and personality characteristics that are distinctive to that character and what motivates them in each scene of the screenplay. Is this likely to assume a position of leadership in particular situations? Do they fade into the background? Is the character a pessimist, optimist, caregiver, jokester, narcissist?

Aligning Characters with Theme

The characters you develop should be directly in line with the story you strive to tell and the story's message. What is that story about, and how does each person involved play a part in bringing it to fruition? When you develop your logline, you ultimately are deciding on the theme of your story as well. How do your characters align with that theme, and how do their actions influence how the reader or audience perceives the theme? There must be characters who are in conflict with the central question and who have to experience a significant change in themselves to realize the answer.

Establishing Interest and Empathy

It is important to draw all qualities of a character together to determine the voice they take throughout the screenplay. You must be sure to maintain a level of empathy and fascination with each character. As you plan out each of your characters, ask yourself the question: what makes this character interesting? Going back to Annie and Blaire's story, let's imagine the thing that makes Annie interesting is the way she writes poems about people on the subway and values her career as a poet above everything else.

Annie is willing to sacrifice sleep, food, and stability in the pursuit of poetry, and she shows persistence in the way she will stop at nothing to get there. Imagine that Blaire is cool-headed and stumbled into success without meaning to. She has an electrifying presence that draws people to her like magnets and keeps them there. When it comes to the empathy piece, you should be sure that each of your characters has some sort of reason or motive for the things they do. Even if your character makes a poor choice or addresses the story's antagonist, there should be some level to which the reader or audience members feel they can understand. There should be something that has happened to the characters who do bad things or make poor decisions that explain why that character does what they do (even when it is unjustified).

Show, Don't Tell

When it comes to character development, you must be able to show, not merely tell. Say to the reader that a particular character is kind and generous but never demonstrates any situations in which they choose to give of themselves to others or treat other people with kindness. There will be no credibility established between the reader and that character. In each line of dialogue, a particular character speaks, their motivations should be clear, and the actions they take should be even more precise. Remember, when it comes to screenwriting, actors will eventually perform physical actions on stage. Be sure to write to accommodate this.

Defining Character Purpose

As you develop your characters, ask yourself the purpose that character exists for in the story's scheme. Do you have a depressed mother who lives to show parents' reality trying their best for their children and yet still struggling to rise above? Is the daughter character someone who learns to demonstrate compassion towards her mother's character, despite the injustices of having an absent parent?

Or does the child assume an attitude of defiance, decide to end the relationship, and promptly leave her mother one day? Each character's position in each scene should contain a more profound message, truth, or perspective that is shown to the audience through the action and dialogue of that character.

Character Archetypes

When it comes to the details of character development, it is essential to consider character archetypes. A caregiving character, for example, is not going to be the selfish character of the story. They are likely to be kind, nurturing, and there to support other characters throughout the screenplay. These are believable actions for them to take. In contrast, selfish, narcissistic, or cruel actions are not reasonable and may throw the reader or audience members off if they are overused. For each character, you develop and write out a full character description, including how that particular character is related to the protagonist and what role they have on the protagonist. It is a good idea to sketch out your characters ahead of time and read over them several times until you have developed the most exciting plot points and conflicts possible.

Use of Dialogue

One of the most distinguishing factors of screenwriting as compared to other types of writing is the use of dialogue. Through dialogue, readers and audience members come to fully understand the characters and what they serve to represent within the screenplay's message.

As you develop how your characters will orient in dialogue, keep in mind the power of various speech patterns and speaking styles. It is essential to imagine all of the details of how actors should speak when portraying particular characters. What speed do they speak at? What are their tone and inflection? Do they have a specific catchphrase?

Just as human beings are unique and have different backgrounds, upbringing, and perspectives, so should your characters. Dialogue is the tool through which you will demonstrate various upbringings and perspectives as your screenplay unfolds. A young male gymnast in Russia, a child who lives in New York and spends her days being a caretaker for her siblings, an older woman who loved through the Great Depression and now lives in a retirement home in the suburbs, a woman who has grown up in a tribe in the Amazon rainforest, and a man living at a mental hospital after being disowned by his family will all have very different ways of speaking, viewing the world, and ultimately, influencing the track of the story. When you develop character dialogue, it should represent the place that a person comes from, the time period, and the things they experienced in their past.

Providing a Back Story

The dialogue between characters should serve to provide readers and audience members with necessary information about the character's backstories. Through dialogue, the audience members should come to understand what motivates the characters to react the way they do. Your audience members should be able to walk away after production and describe how a particular character would respond in a hypothetical situation. If you have ever had conversations with your friends about "If I were a character from _____ who would I be?" that screenwriter did an excellent job of creating distinguished characters with whom you could establish a connection and demonstrate your understanding of that character's personality.

Using Monologue

If your screenplay uses monologue at any point, it is vital to make it stick out. Monologues are most useful when they demonstrate some elements of character development. An example of this would be if Annie realized she was in an abusive relationship, had a monologue with herself one night in the shower, came to the realization that she had to escape, and then found a way to do so. This demonstrates the development of her character, as she finds the strength and courage to leave, as well as the development of the story as a whole.

Distinguishing your Characters

When characters are engaging in dialogue in a particular scene, there must be distinguishing factors that allow you to understand who is speaking. Well-developed characters are characters the audience member can identify simply by their style of speaking and their approach.

As you design your characters and determine what distinguishes them from one another, try to quiz yourself by covering up character names and seeing if you can identify who is who simply by their actions and how they engage in dialogue. Once you can do this, you can be sure that you have developed complex characters who each serve a purpose and are necessary to the story in their own right.

Using Character Complexity to Create Surprise

Another benefit of developing complex characters is that there is more potential for shock value. Does the person experience a mid-life crisis that leads them to flee home and go across the country? Are they kind throughout most of the play and then end up having a breakdown and become evil? Or perhaps they start out evil and have a change of heart. Whatever the case may be, you can use characters and how they change throughout a show to connect your audience to the message further and surprise them throughout.

Crafting Multi-Dimensional Characters

One last thing to keep in mind when it comes to character development is that the characters you develop should have many dimensions, just as human beings do. Think of yourself on a given day. You may have a great day one day, where you are joyful in everything you do, engage in meaningful conversations, fulfill all of your obligations, and treat people with kindness. The next day, you may be anxious, or angry, absentminded, or simply unable to keep up with everything going on. We all have good days and bad days, and dimensions to our personality which impact how we act in a given social scenario. The characters you develop in your screenplays should be just as complex. What are the traits that are characteristic of them, and what features are uncharacteristic and symbolize that something is off? Make sure to establish these things early on in the character development process. What is the mood of each character in each scene, and how does it change throughout?

Tips for Character Writing

One of the best tips for character development is to develop a personal connection with the characters. Many successful screenwriters dedicate a lot of time to considering all the possibilities of personality traits that may exist within a given character and how that character may react in certain life situations. They do this so much that they eventually reach a point where they feel like they know the character on a personal level.

Another option is to brainstorm a variety of characterizations based upon major life events each character endures. In some cases, it can help draw inspiration for personality or physical appearance based on other characters you have seen or other people you have known. If you have a photo to use as a "model" of your character, this can also be helpful.

Another standard method is to write character outlines or create diagrams that demonstrate how multi-faceted characters are. Suppose you're writing about an antagonist who originally comes off as a kind person and an ally. In that case, you may create a bubble map diagram in which the character's name is in the middle, and branching off from that are other bubbles with characteristics such as "manipulative," "deceptive," "sneaky," "dishonest," "intelligent," etc. all which lead to the tactics this character uses to appear reasonable while working towards their harmful agenda.

Crafting Character Biographies

Character Biography is an excellent tool to make use of when it comes to character development. This writing exercise helps you develop your characters' history from the day they were born until the moment your story starts. What forces have acted on that character's life to bring them to where they are? Did anything happen during their earlier years that led them to adopt certain behaviors? Just as every person you meet has an entire story that has led them into that moment, so should the characters you develop.

Trace that character's journey all the way back to when and where they were born. Who were they born to, and how did their family history impact what sort of situation they were taken into? What city or country were they born into, and have they had to move to a new one or watched the one they always knew undergoing changes? Is the character born male or female? Do they act in particularly gendered ways? Did they have a healthy relationship with their parents? Did their parents have a healthy relationship with each other? How do they align or not align with what is expected of them culturally, concerning gender, etc.?

Did they grow up with siblings or as only children? If they did, what was their relationship like with their siblings? What challenges or successes did they have in school or with extracurriculars? Did they have physical, psychological, or emotional struggles? What did your character learn from the people they grew up around? Have they experienced a traumatic event of any kind? When the story begins, how much life has your character lived? How old are they? Have they moved around or lived in virtually the same place their entire life? Were they born in an area that is different from where the story takes place? Have they had a happy, sad, difficult, or relatively easy life leading up to that point?

It is also essential to consider the various elements of personality your characters have demonstrated over the years. What was their relationship with authority? How did they orient in social situations? Were they respectful, goody two shoes who never got in trouble, or were they always making mischief? Were they social and outgoing, or did they prefer to remain reserved? Perhaps they started out as one and then adopted the qualities of another. No matter what you decide, allow yourself to find joy in the process, and be guided by your creativity. It is also okay to draw influence from your personal life or the lives of other people, you know.

Give yourself time to write about ten pages dedicated to several of your main characters' character biographies in various life stages. Answer as many questions as you can about what their life has been like. How has their personality developed over the years? What strengths and challenges do they face daily, and how does that impact their role in the screenplay events? What are their relationships with other friends, family members, coworkers, teachers, etc.? If the character you are writing about is not the protagonist, what is their relationship to the protagonist? What kind of light do they shed on the main character? If they are the protagonist, what is their relationship to the other people in their lives?

Getting in the Right Head Space

Representing the human experience through character development is not an easy task, and it can take time to develop a personal connection with your characters. Give yourself a few days to ponder your potential characters, writing down ideas you have as you go. Dedicate a few hours of undistracted time to brainstorming ideas of how that character might orient in the story. It is important not to judge yourself or be too rigid in the development during the brainstorming process, as it is the part where you simply get to let all of your ideas out without judgment or stipulations. The critical factor here is simply getting your ideas down and coming to know your characters on a personal level. Allow yourself to free write as the characters discover themselves. Who are they in the individual, private, and professional environments of their lives?

Allow yourself to have fun describing the things your character likes and dislikes. What are their passions? What do they like to eat and drink? What is their occupation, and do they like it? What are their current relationships like? In some cases, you may benefit from designing a "day in the life" for your characters and trying to make them as detailed as possible. Allow yourself to discover the characters as you go, much like you would discover yourself or the people you interact with daily.

Think of this as a relationship-building process, like you would experience when dating or building a friendship. You should feel such a connection to your characters by the end that they are like friends or family to you.

Chapter 3: Step 3 - Expanding your Screenplay Through Plot

When it comes to all of the screenplays that exist in the world, it is no surprise that your plot must have things that distinguish it from the rest. When developing character journeys, challenges, and obstacles, you have to be able to think outside the box and go against what people expect. These journeys, challenges, and obstacles look different depending on the screenplay genre, but they must always begin with an inciting incident. As mentioned earlier, the inciting incident is the triggering event that serves as the catalyst into the tensest and action-packed part of the screenplay.

This initial action in the plot is like the doorway that opens and invites the audience into the rest of the story. It is full of surprises and challenges as the conflict unfolds around the protagonist, and the protagonist has to figure out how to address it. At first, the protagonist may feel some resistance to dealing with the obstacle they face. The inciting incident has to be something that takes them out of their comfort zone and causes them to feel hesitant about what to do next. However, the environment must eventually become so high-stakes that they have no choice but to act.

Making your Audience Care

To establish this high-stakes environment, you have to make your audience care about the character and what is happening to them from the very beginning. There is no time to waste; you must immediately establish the emotional connection between your audience and the characters. Help them establish a feeling of hatred, love, or fascination with the character and how life unfolds around them. You have to be prepared to hit the ground running, bringing your reader in so far that once you reach the inciting event, nothing can draw their attention away from what is happening. After you have set this precedent and introduced your inciting incident, you will have established a substantial focus for the rest of your story.

Imagine you are writing a story about a young girl who is learning she has psychic powers. You can immediately engage your audience by establishing a feeling of fascination as they watch the young girl realize she can tell what will happen before it does. She may know that a family of six will move into the house down the street, that the neighbor man will ask her single mother out on a date, that she will see four hummingbirds in the garden one morning, and even that her teacher will be in a car accident on the way to school one day. This builds up the level of fascination within the audience and brings them to the inciting incident.

Setting the First Act

The initial precedent-setting and inciting incident are elements of the First Act, where you must seize your audience and keep them engaged. The central conflict in this part of the screenplay keeps the audience on the edge of their seat, anxious to see what happens in the Second Act. By the end of the First Act, the audience should be very clear on the protagonist's main goals and what is standing in their way.

In the case of the screenplay described, the inciting incident happens one day when the girl gets a terrible feeling in the pit of her stomach and knows that her mother will be fired. Sure enough, when her mother comes into the house that afternoon, her eyes are puffy from crying. This inciting incident leads the girl and her mother to leave the city they're living in and move across the country to live in New York, the place her mother has always dreamt of going. Once the girl and her mother have moved to New York, they face several conflicts, from having someone break into their apartment one night to having roaches and rats in the kitchen, all of which the young girl predicts with her psychic powers. As things continue to go wrong throughout the first act, the young girl becomes increasingly miserable because she can't understand her strengths and doesn't know who to speak to about them. The girl's primary goal is to understand her abilities and learn how to live with them and use them for good.

Introducing Additional Conflicts in the Second Act

Once the First Act Break is over, the protagonist will enter into a place of additional conflicts that pose difficulty to their main goals and bring them towards the climax. At this point, the audience should be able to pinpoint multiple conflicts the protagonist has faced. At the Midpoint region, the character is thrust into an even more challenging situation than they had dealt with previously, and they will have to act differently. This is the point where things seem bad, and the audience will be forced to wonder if the protagonist will end up on top or not. At this point of tension, the Second Act Break will occur. This is when the protagonist has made the realizations and changes they need to make to push the story towards its climax.

The Midpoint region of this particular screenplay could be that the young girl wakes up one morning with the suspicion that there will be a terrible accident on the subway her mother takes to work in the morning. The girl feels desperate to save her mother, and she tears out of her bedroom, only to find her mother has left the house early. The girl finds a note on the kitchen table that reads, "went to the coffee shop down the road before work. Have whatever you want for breakfast; I'll see you soon." The girl tears out of the house and down the street, peering into every coffee shop on her way to the subway system. Her heart is pounding, and the audience doesn't know whether or not she will find her mother.

Tying up the Story with Climax

The climax is the part of the story where everything is tied together, and it becomes clear why everything has happened to lead the protagonist to this point. They have a final confrontation with the central conflict and typically end up on top.

In this story's climax, the young girl races through the city until she finds the subway station where her mother gets on the subway to go to work. She rushes down the stairs and arrives just as the L Train stops and passengers are getting on. The girl sees her mother and begins to scream, "STOP! STOP! There is going to be a terrible accident! Everyone get off the subway!" Most people in the station look at her like she is crazy, but her mother recognizes her voices and turns to face her. Her mother becomes so shocked that she is there that she does not get on the subway.

Instead, the two unite, and the girl begins screaming that they need to leave immediately. They do, and no sooner have they stepped out of the subway than a massive fire breaks out on the tracks.

After this, the rest of the story involves the young girl coming clean to her mother about her powers and beginning to use her psychic nature for good to help the people around her in any way she can (without revealing herself).

Chapter 4: Step 4 - Generating the First Draft

One of the most crucial things to keep in mind when it comes to screenwriting is that your first draft will take on many forms throughout the process of its creation. The first draft exists primarily for your personal use, in truly narrowing down your screenplay's goal and ensuring everything is expressed clearly. Your first draft does not need to embody the final product's wholeness, as long as it contains the essential elements such as theme, plot, and characters. Your first draft can be as basic or as concrete as you wish,

but no matter what, you must be aware that it is not designed to be the final product.

One of the most important things to remember when generating your first draft is this: it is not designed for your intended audience. When you send it out, it should be sent only to those whose advice you trust most, with the knowledge that it will continue to evolve. Allow yourself to take plenty of breaks from the draft, giving yourself a few days to think about other things before looking at it again. You mustn't rush your process. At the end of the day, the first draft's goal is not that it be perfectly polished, but instead that it provides a solid framework on which to build.

Establishing Basic Intentions

As you begin the process of writing your first draft, you should be able to describe the basics of who your characters are, what they want, the obstacles they will face, and the ultimate theme of your story. It is a good idea to start your process with a piece of paper dedicated to your plot, characters, and theme. On each piece of paper, write down your intentions for each of these elements. You can continue to refer back to these pieces of paper throughout your writing process to ensure you stay on track with what you want to express and how you want to express it. It is normal to find that you are straying slightly from your original intentions throughout the screenwriting process. Do not allow this to discourage you—instead, check-in with yourself.

Ask if your intentions still hold or if the story's development and characters take on a mind of their own and lead you towards new purposes. It is certainly okay to adapt your intentions as needed throughout the process of writing your rough draft. The biggest thing you must pay attention to if your intentions shift is that they are all moving in the same direction, so you can make an executive decision to change the intentions without leading certain parts of the screenplay astray.

Writing Detailed Characters

As you plan out your characters, it is crucial to write out all of the details that make them who they are, even if those details are not revealed in the script itself. Even if your audience does not know all of the details of your character's family life, relationship history, favorite things to do, or places where they draw the most joy and inspiration in their life, you should know. You should be able to answer questions about your characters from the most mundane details, like what they like to eat for breakfast, to the profound details, like the dream that they will never reveal to anyone because they see it as impossible. By planning out all of these details ahead of time, you will develop a more real and personal relationship with your characters, and you will find it easier to maintain consistency in their actions and dialogue.

Layering Character Representation

When it comes to characterization, it is essential to ask yourself if these characters are being represented the way you planned for them to be. Are you staying true to their personality traits with the actions they take in each scene? Are the ways they interact with others characteristic of who they are? What are their flaws, challenges, motivations, and goals? How do they fulfill the expectations the audience has of them? How do they veer away from those expectations to surprise the audience?

Throughout the first draft writing process, it is customary to see your characters developing more layers than you initially expected; you may even find that your intentions for each character shift. The first draft writing process is a chance to bring your characters to life, and you may be surprised at the decisions they make and the way they inhabit the story. If you need to, allow yourself to break from the script's goals and write out all of the possible reactions your characters could have to a particular scenario. Give yourself the space to flesh out all of the ways they might feel or react. As you go through this process, try to put yourself in each character's shoes and write from their perspective rather than your own.

Staying True to the Theme

In terms of theme, one of the best ways to keep yourself focused is to ask questions. An excellent question to keep you on track is: What do I want my audience to take forward from this screenplay? Continue referring back to this question as you go, ensuring that what is currently happening will ultimately lead to the desired impact. As you write out the scenes within your plot, be sure to examine the overarching theme of that particular scene and ask yourself how it leads the audience towards a conclusion. How does it make them think? What emotions will it invoke within them? What will they learn?

Taking it Slow

It's easy to lose sight of what you wish to express by giving the first and second acts plenty of time but then beginning to rush as you reach the climax and the conclusion. This can leave the audience feeling deeply dissatisfied and like too much has happened too quickly for them to truly generate an opinion. If you begin to feel desperate to get done but don't have any fresh ideas, allow yourself to take a step back.

Writing the end of your screenplay from a place of urgency and pressure will lead to sloppiness and will inevitably leave the audience feeling unfulfilled. Give yourself time to step away and clear your mind so you can be more thorough and make fewer mistakes when you come back to it. Give yourself a refresher with your initial intentions and ideas. Ask yourself if another film, book, song, or podcast may re-inspire you and remind you why you wanted to write this particular screenplay. It is imperative to give this process adequate time to unfold and refrain from rushing yourself as you start to get closer to the end. Taking this time to refresh yourself early on can save a lot of headaches later, and you'll ultimately be glad you stepped away for a while.

Making Use of Free-Writing

After you have established initial intentions, it's an excellent idea to free-write using a pen and paper or a blank document on your computer. Allow all of the images and possibilities for your characters to flow out freely, without judgment. It may seem strange, but one of the crucial tips for screenwriting is to write the ridiculous and confusing dialogue, unpolished scenes, and random character descriptions. Writing the lousy stuff first makes editing more manageable later on because you have less confusion to work through since you took time to iron out the details beforehand.

Additionally, the more material you have to work with initially, the more potential your screenplay holds. Work through all of your ideas, and see if you can find any common themes. Which images are the strongest? Which connections can you make between them? What opportunities exist for meaningful dialogue? After you have gotten all of your thoughts out, allow yourself to look at them more critically, checking for clarity and being particular about which ideas you qualify to make it into your script. The more ideas you have to choose from, the more likely it is that your script will be fresh and provide something producers, managers, and directors have never seen before.

Setting Attainable Goals

As you write your first draft, it is good to set goals to keep yourself on track. One of your goals may be to write one scene per day so that you can approach each new writing session with a fresh perspective, ready to address the purposes of a new scene. Another goal may be to learn something new from each scene you write and be inspired by the way your script is taking form. You may set a goal to finish writing a scene in a particular amount of time or with a specific tone of the dialogue. Although daily goalsetting is crucial for staying on track, make sure not to overshoot with your goals. Give yourself goals that you can reasonably achieve.

Making Use of Treatments and Loglines

Earlier in this guide, we discussed the fact that a logline is a great way to keep you on track with your script's goals. It is the element that allows you to describe using less than thirty words what your screenplay is all about. This concise summary of what your play is about can be a great reminder to keep you on track as you go throughout the writing process. However, just as there is room for your rough draft to grow and change, there is room for your logline to change along with it. You have to change your logline's wording to summarize your story adequately, especially if you find that your intentions have changed. Allow yourself to make these changes to your logline as needed to stay true to your core intentions and fully capture everything you want to express in your screenplay.

Developing a Treatment

Another useful element of keeping your first draft on track is through developing a treatment. The treatment serves as a more extensive summary of your script's plot, themes, and characters, and it helps bring clarity to these elements. Once you have narrowed down your initial intentions, you can write a piece of prose consisting of several sentences that summarize what those intentions are. The treatment stands between your initial intentions and the actual script and allows you to clarify without becoming distracted by too many extra details. The treatment is brief but provides a little more insight into your particular intentions. In writing this, you can clarify each of your intentions and provide yourself with an objective summation to go back to as you continue to write your first draft. The treatment should contain all the clarification you need to keep yourself from losing sight of where you want to go.

One of the best things about the first draft is that you have the freedom to place as much dialogue as you want. You can allow your characters to talk, however, and about whatever seems fit for a particular scene. However, it is essential to remember that much of the dialogue you write initially will change if it stays in at all.

Fleshing Out Dialogue

As you write your first draft, allow yourself to play into all of the possibilities of dialogue. Inhabit the space of your character's conversations, leaving room for messiness and confusion. What mindsets can you capture using dialogue? Save the cutting and editing of dialogue for the revision process. Once you get to the revision of the first draft, you will have more possibilities to sift through to decide what makes the cut. When it comes time to edit, be prepared to make many cuts to keep the script moving forward in line with the plot, theme, and character goals. If the audience gets lost in the dialogue and things begin to stall, you risk losing their attention.

Maintaining Flexibility

Your first draft is something that should be written with the idea that more versions will arise from it. The first draft is not meant to be even close to the end all be all of your screenplays. Therefore, you should give yourself the freedom to enjoy the process, writing your ideas, and seeing where they lead you. Do not write from a place of tension or pressure to get everything right because that is unrealistic and may slow you down or prohibit you from achieving the revelations that come in letting yourself run free. There is no set number of how many drafts you will produce before you finally reach the end, but you should expect to produce no less than three. Any less than three drafts will leave you feeling nervous, and like there are still ways the draft could improve. Remember, the first draft is only the first step of the journey.

Chapter 5: Step 5 - Crafting your Pitch Deck

As screenwriting has become more competitive over the years, the way screenplays are pitched has changed dramatically. While loglines, synopses, and treatments are still crucial elements of pitching a script, more details are required to succeed in the pitching process. All of these elements combine to create what is called a pitch deck. While the logline is the first thing producers, managers, agents, and development executives will be exposed to with your screenplay, the pitch deck is the thing that will help them go beyond.

Capturing their attention with the logline is only the first part of the process. From there, you must craft a pitch deck which is highly creative, visually engaging, and full of just enough detail and information to make them interested and help them visualize how the story will be told (too much information is not a good idea, as they will quickly lose interest). The pitch deck is the make it or break it factor when it comes to whether or not people will choose to invest in your screenplay. You have to show them why you deserve their investment, what will make your project worth it, and, ultimately, what is in it for them.

When it comes to outlining your pitch deck, you must have each of the following sections: Title page, executive summary, team, story, production, distribution, and finances. Each of these elements will be broken down in further detail.

Catching Attention with a Title Page

The title page will serve as the cover of your pitch and should contain qualities of a poster or similar visual aid. You can share contact information on this title page for producers, managers, agents, and development executives to refer back to. This poster should utilize a color scheme, font, and images that capture your screenplay's tone and atmosphere. You would not, for example, want to use a horror style font on a title page for a romance screenplay.

Providing an Executive Summary

Your pitch deck's executive summary should be one page long and should include your pitch's primary elements. Some crucial information to include is the title, genre, how long the screenplay will be, the proposed budget, and what dates shooting should take place (if it is a film).

Introducing the Team

This section of the pitch deck should include who the prominent team members of the project will be. Team members include attached development executives or producers, yourself, and any co-writers, as well as potential writers, directors, producers, or lead actors if you are pitching a film. Each team member should be complete with an image and a biography.

Telling the Story

To successfully pitch a screenplay, you must be able to provide summarize the protagonist's story and the most important details of their character in a brief but engaging way. Show the reader why they should care about this character and their journey, and how the rest of the world can be impacted. The story element of the pitch deck is the part that includes your logline, which briefly presents your lead protagonist's background and the conflicts they face.

Describing Production

One of the significant parts of the production element is proving to the readers that there are benefits to producing this type of play or film. You can use factors such as demographics, popular interest areas of the general public, current events, etc. This section should also include when and where production will take place.

Building on Distribution

This section gives you a chance to continue building on why this particular genre is needed in the industry and will therefore be a worthwhile investment. Use this section to continue talking about demographics, as well as potential distributors.

Stating Finances

Most projects require money to get off the ground. You must include a breakdown of all anticipated costs for your proposed play or film so that directors, producers, and managers have an idea ahead of time of what their money will be going to.

Final Reminders

There are a few essential things to keep in mind as you develop your pitch deck. The first is to summarize the protagonist's story and the most important details of their character in a brief but engaging way.

Show the reader why they should care about this character and their journey, and how the rest of the world can be impacted by it. Next, your pitch deck must serve to provide the reader with instantly discernable clues. You must use visual, descriptive language, which will paint a picture in the reader's mind of how the screenplay will appear on stage or the screen. Logistically, you need to include complete details about targeted genres, demographics, and financial allocations. You will know your pitch deck has done its job if the reader walks away with an idea of the screenplay's story, character arc, tone, theme, scope, as well as financial and production logistics.

Chapter 6: Step 6 - Rewriting for Refinement

As discussed in the First Draft chapter of this guide, the best scripts are that writers take time away from and then examine with fresh eyes. Screenwriting is exhausting, and it can quickly become muddled. One of the best screenwriting tips is to give yourself at least a week, if not several weeks, of not doing it. Give yourself time to go on a vacation, read a book you've been dying to read, spend some time outside, watch a film or play written by someone else, spend time with loved ones, nap, or anything else you love to do. Allow yourself to clear your mind and pay serious attention to the things happening around you. When you go back to continue the screenwriting process, bring the perspectives you have gathered out in the world back with you. Read your script with fresh eyes, as if you have never seen it before. Be critical in the same way a reader would be, looking for what it is that makes this particular script stand out.

Cutting the Fat

As you work your way through the structure, allow yourself to be ruthless. Toss out the things that do not work out well, and make sure that each scene sets a precedent for what will happen next. Tie up loose ends and clean up messy, unclear areas. Speak the lines of dialogue out loud. Consider the setting dialogue is unfolding in—how does it contribute to the shape of the dialogue and the visual representation on stage or the screen? Check back with the fascination you built at the beginning of the story to measure if your climax is intense and surprising enough. Ask yourself what the audience should get out of this, and make sure their expectations are met.

Developing Compelling Characters and Conflicts

One major mistake to look out for is unengaging characters or conflicts. If your main character is boring and does not keep you engaged, ask yourself what sort of compelling backstory you may be able to give them that might make them more attractive. In the case of the girl with the psychic powers, perhaps an exciting subplot would be that she has previously felt useless and dull as if she brings nothing of much value to the world. This backstory keeps things interesting and retains the character experiencing an element of surprise and rooting for her throughout. In terms of conflict, make sure that it is something that profoundly impacts the character's life. Set the stakes as high as possible, and make sure they are clear and ever-increasing.

In the girl's story with the psychic powers, the stakes reach an all-time high at the climax when her mother is about to lose her life. At this point, the girl's motivations are clear, convincing, and capturing—she must save her mother.

If you find yourself struggling with the story's depth or how the plot unfolds, it may be time to check in with consistency. Ask yourself if the characters are consistent with their intended motivations or how they perceive themselves. Are the instances of each scene engaging but also believable? Can the audience understand why certain things are happening?

Use tools like flashbacks, narrations, or dreams to keep things moving and keep the story from going flat. At the same time, be sure to avoid using too much narrative. If the scenes are too busy telling to show what is happening, the scene will be weak. The goal should be for the scene to be so strong that dialogue can take any shape within it, and the audience will still have an idea of what is going on and what the purpose is.

Avoiding Monotony and Wordiness

Another common mistake to avoid is monotony in the dialogue. This does not have to do with how the lines are being said and the nature of the dialogue. Dialogue should vary from person to person, and each character's lines should be characteristic of their personality and their goals. Remember that character is best shown through action, not through dull recitations of history or exposition.

It is crucial to avoid being too wordy. Every time you approach the rewriting process, you should do so to cut words out of every dialogue and every scene. You should cut the phrases down so far that you are only one word away from the phrase, no longer making sense.

If you are not concise, audience members will become lost in the telling of the story. Remember to show, don't tell. How many words can be replaced by actions?

Avoiding Repetition

If things start to become too repetitive and you find certain scenes or characters being too much like another, take a minute to step back. What are the unique personalities and voices of each character? If you have several of almost the same personality or voice, perhaps consider combining them to create fewer, more interesting characters. Adjust your scene length as needed—if a scene becomes too long, it will begin to seem like everything has already been seen or heard, and it will lose its appeal.

Dealing with Lengthy Scripts

If the script itself is too long, it is time to start looking for areas where you may be repeating yourself. If you have the same information in the script multiple times, it is safe to say it can be cut. You can reiterate information by the actions the characters take, as opposed to having to say it over and over. Check all of your subplots and make sure you are not going in too many directions and trying to cover too much.

Lengthening Scripts When Needed

If the script is too short, it may be a sign that your characters are underdeveloped. You may be lacking a subplot. In the psychic girl and her mother's story, there is room to integrate the subplots about the girl's emotional issues and perhaps her mother's long-time loneliness as a single mother. This adds a sense of depth to the story and gives a lot of room for further development. Be sure not to sacrifice character complexity to keep the plot moving. It is essential to strike a balance.

Reaching out to Proofreaders

Once you've reached the perceived end of your rewriting process, reach out to several people whose opinions you deeply trust. Listen to the way they perceive the screenplay and what advice they give. You do not have to agree with their perspective, but you should take it seriously. Allow yourself to polish repeatedly until the script is no longer improving; it is merely changing forms. Once you reach this point, you're ready.

Chapter 7: Step 7 - Applying the Secrets of Distinguished Screenplay Writing

There are several secrets that every screenwriter should know to create the most engaging, impactful screenplays in the industry. This chapter will serve as a recap of several essential tips to make your screenplay stick out above all the rest.

Fueling Dialogue Through Action and Reaction

As we have already discussed, the best way to draw your audience into a screenplay is to show, don't tell. One great way to do this is to imagine that you are writing a silent movie in which none of the characters can speak. This does not take away the power of dialogue—quite the contrary. Instead, it fuels the dialogue by adding actions and reactions to deliver with the lines. Suppose one character is antagonizing another, and the other character pulls out a gun. In that case, that will inevitably have more power than the character merely saying, "Stand back, or I'll shoot," and taking no action. From this action and reaction, the audience learns that there is great tension between these two characters, and one of them is not afraid to take the other's life away right then and there. Suppose a character dreams of being a famous dancer. In that case, the audience will get more of a sense of her motivation by watching scenes where she dances in her bedroom every night before bed instead of listening to a monologue about how much she cares about dance.

Screenwriting is distinguished from other types of writing in that the content you create is designed to take on physical form on the stage or screen. For this reason, action is crucial to keep the audience engaged with what is happening before them. Think about the events that unfold around you in everyday life. What a bland and confusing world it would be if people did not use facial expressions and other actions along with their words! In many circumstances, it is the nonverbal things that truly express what another person is feeling. By providing actions, facial expressions, and other physical representations along with the dialogue, you can be sure to keep your audience feeling connected to the characters and "reading into" their actions to determine what may happen next.

Determining what Needs to be Said

With every line of dialogue, it is important to look critically and ask if what is being said truly needs to be said or if it can be shown instead. If there is no full reason for it to be said, it is best to cut it out. If you do not find it necessary, neither will the audience. Your dialogue's entire goal should be that it is easy for the audience members to follow along without becoming bored or distracted. Dialogue should accomplish one primary goal: to progress towards the motivation of the protagonist. As you go through your rewriting process, cut your dialogue down as far as it can go.

Make sure that each line of dialogue is serving as a building block to construct the larger picture. With every scene of dialogue, build to the climax and back it up with actions.

Keeping Supporting Characters in their Place

Another tip to keep in mind in terms of character dialogue is not giving lines to the wrong characters. Supporting characters exist for that reason: to support the narrative surrounding the protagonist's goals. Do not make the mistake of having characters talk simply because they are present in a scene. In many cases, it is powerful enough to have a particular character walking around, in silent dialogue with another character, doing their job, etc. while the main dialogue takes place aside from them. Each line of dialogue must serve the purpose of moving the plot and characters forward, and this purpose is defeated if characters are talking just for the sake of talking.

Supporting characters are there to help the lead characters, and they should not speak unless it accomplishes that goal. If their line does not contribute to moving the screenplay forward, the line should be cut. Not all characters in the room need to have a line, and in fact, there is a specific power in having characters present in a scene who say nothing at all.

Concealing Character Desires

A significant way to keep the audience on the edge of their seats is by never giving away what the characters want deep down inside. While the screenwriter should always know the character's goals, motivations, and desires, these things should never be explicitly stated to the audience. Rather, the audience is left to draw their own conclusions about what the characters are striving for by listening to what they say and looking for deeper meanings. The dialogue should never truly reveal what the characters want until the end. This keeps characters guessing and open for discovery, and they will listen more intentionally as they try to crack the code.

"Movie Moments": Speaking Power in Dialogue

One mistake that screenwriters commonly make in writing dialogue is the attempt to make it sound "real." In reality, the best dialogue should not resemble an everyday conversation. The best dialogue should take the powerful form of what people wish they could say but can't. Robust dialogue should not include stuttering or filler words, and it should not go off on tangents. Instead, it should capture raw emotion and be short, assertive ideas that stick with the reader.

Although it is important to include human moments like fragments and interruptions, cinematic dialogue should be impactful, engaging, and sometimes even poetic in nature. As you craft your dialogue, consider what film phrases have become most popular and stuck with people worldwide.

When it comes to writing conflict, you must remember that the best dispute arises from two or more characters with vastly different goals and desires. The conflict should tie itself into every dialogue, which will cause the audience to be engaged with the back and forth, curious to see who is going to come out on top. Inevitably, the audience will agree with one character more than the others and will begin subconsciously rooting for that character's success. Going back to the young girl's story with psychic powers, let's imagine that after her mother comes home from work after being fired and says they need to move, the girl tries to convince her mother otherwise.

At the time, the girl's mother does not know of her daughter's powers and therefore doesn't understand that her daughter is trying to dissuade her from moving because she has a feeling something terrible will happen if they do. The two will go back and forth about why they should or should not move, and at the climax, this discourse will be enhanced by the fact that the little girl turned out to be right— her mother is in grave danger.

Drawing Inspiration from Other Screenwriters

One of the most important things to do is to read other screenplays when it comes to being a good screenwriter. In many cases, writing is all about the inspiration we draw from the most brilliant and successful voices in the field, and screenwriting is no exception to this. Half the battle of being a successful screenwriter is becoming familiar with other people who have already done it.

As you read the work of successful screenwriters, you will inevitably be exposed to stylistic choices, tactics, and approaches that are most inspirational and impactful to the audience. As you read work that inspires you, you are likely to become more inclined to create your work and feel motivated to create something that can impact the world. Frequently, reading other screenwriters' work is just the jumpstart you need to motivate yourself to start your masterpiece. You can experiment with different styles, voices, points of view, dialogic interactions, and character-building techniques based upon what inspires you from the work of others.

Screenplays, especially free screenplays, are like gold to the aspiring screenwriter. Within the thousands of scripts you can dig into, you will discover new ways of crafting dialogue, writing elements of surprise, and keeping your reader emotionally engaged. If you want to improve as a screenwriter, making yourself an apprentice to other screenwriters' work through reading is the best way to do so.

All it takes to engage with thousands of free screenplays is the desire to find them. These screenplays can be found in collections online, and a vast number of them are available with no fees attached. As you read the work of the screenwriters who inspire you most, allow yourself to channel their genius and let it flow into your writing. Artists exist to encourage one another and create a never-ending cycle of creativity, and this is something every screenwriter should use to their advantage.

Conclusion

When you started this guide, you had an interest in screenwriting and the desire to build skills to set yourself apart in the industry. Throughout the guide, you were provided with the ins and outs of screenwriting, how to distinguish your style, characters, and ideas.

You learned how to keep your audience engaged, write meaningful dialogue, and follow a proper screenwriting model. You also learned things to avoid and tips to keep your creativity flowing freely. You discovered how to draw in your readers and keep them engaged and inspire them to invest in your screenplay to bring it to the stage or screen.

You learned how to write a script in an actionable way that is easily transferable to a physical setting, such as a screen or stage. With this, you understood how to keep your readers engaged in the real-world human interactions occurring between the characters. You also came to understand the power that lies in screenwriting and what sets it apart from other writing types.

At the end of the guide, you were provided with expert tips to keep your screenplays fresh and avoid the common mistakes made by amateurs in the industry. You learned how to develop a dialogue to avoids unnecessary details and focus on action. You learned how to determine what needs to be said, and what can simply be inferred through character action and nonverbal cues.

You learned which characters to emphasize and how to avoid the protagonist's focus and their primary goal. Additionally, you realized the importance of reading other screenwriters' work, drawing inspiration, and channeling their power as you develop your personal style, voice, and goals with the screenplays you produce. You began this journey by uncovering the purpose of the story being told all of screenplay writing's technicalities: developing characters, inciting incidents, goals, and an eventual resolution.

You discovered the importance of thorough character development and the use of dialogue, plot development using scenes, and the process of writing drafts and revising to tie everything together. You learned the importance of giving your drafts space and taking time to walk away from the script to allow further creativity to spark new ideas.

You learned how to hook readers and keep them engaged throughout, as well as how to invoke an emotional experience. Additionally, you were provided with comprehensive tips and tricks to help you distinguish yourself as a screenwriter and keep yourself from getting overwhelmed with the process. You learned several key terms and logistical elements of the screenwriting process, as well as tips and tricks for getting your work out in the world and staying there. With this guide nearby as a tool for you to refer back to anytime throughout your screenwriting process if you get stuck, you're ready to begin!

Book 2: How to Tell a Story

7 Easy Steps to Master Storytelling, Story Boarding, Writing Stories, Storyteller & Story Structure

Jaiden Pemton

Introduction

There is a magic in storytelling that has been present and passed down from generation to generation. When you tell a story, you have the entire world at your fingertips, and you can relay the message to your audience in any way you desire. Storytelling gives you the power to create life-altering emotional experiences for the people reading and listening, and it provides your personal experiences. It values the ability to live on forever.

When it comes to storytelling, it can be easy to get carried away and find your audience feeling lost or not being able to understand the point of the story. It is easy to fall into the trap of including too many details, or not enough, in speaking too long, using the unappealing language for your audience, or creating an emotionally flat story. There are several elements to keep in mind to ensure that your audience is engaged and that your story will live on with them, and be passed on to others for years to come.

Storytelling can seem like a daunting task, especially in today's age, where people have short attention spans and difficulty creating emotional connections to the stories being told to them. That said, there is still hope for storytellers to engage people with what they are saying and for their message to have the desired impact. All it takes is an in-depth knowledge of the storytelling elements that will make your readers and listeners care about what is being told to them and want to stick around for the shining moment.

This guide will serve as your step-by step reference through the realm of storytelling — breaking down the details within each step of the process and helping you to understand what makes your stories essential and how to relay that to your audience.

The chapters of this guide will take you through each step of storytelling in a way that will help you check all the boxes and avoid common mistakes. Together, we will explore the best techniques for developing your plot, knowing your audience, keeping audience engagement levels high, creating an emotional experience for your audience, tying your narrative in to increase levels of empathy, maintaining an element of surprise, and establishing a shining moment which can maintain the test of time. Each detail is designed to keep you on track and answer any questions you may have about the storytelling process. Throughout the journey, you will find yourself discovering the importance of the life experiences you have had that have led you to the point of wanting to tell this story and how you can use your life experience to change your audience's lives.

Each chapter is organized in an easy-to-follow, subtitled format with comprehensive examples of every tip, trick, and technique. This all-inclusive guide to storytelling also contains a few exclusive secrets and information that can help you further develop your skills and create impactful stories.

Whether you are aiming to tell stories directly as they happened in your life, with yourself as the central character, or stories which are loosely based on your experience but center around other characters and a fantasy plot, this guide has all the tools you need and is sure to serve as the perfect guide to revolutionize your storytelling experience.

Happy writing!

Chapter 1: Step 1 - Establishing Purpose and Structure

When it comes to storytelling, it is vital to know the reason you have to tell the story. What makes it essential; what message needs to be relayed to the world through your story? How will this story be unlike anything else, and how will its message speak for itself and stick with the audience?

Defining the Take-Away

Any successful story must begin with a takeaway message. Think back to the stories you have heard in the past that you think of often. Perhaps these are stories that you find yourself re-telling to other people, or always find yourself asking to hear or read again. These are the stories that shape how you approach your daily life—the stories you can never tire of hearing.

To tell a powerful story, you must deliver a message that will have the same long-lasting impact on your audience. You should strive for the stories you tell to be those your audience will apply to their life over and over again. Imagine, for example, your grandfather telling you a story about the bracelet he never takes off, which was given to him by a friend and fellow soldier in World War II. In this story, your grandfather defines the power of friendship as he narrates how he and this man became friends. He includes the conflict and challenges they overcame throughout the war and describes the particular battle in which his friend was shot. With tears in his eyes, he describes the way he felt his heartbreak on the battlefield as his best friend died in his arms. This story's takeaway is the power of friendship and how it persists through challenges and even through a great loss.

Keeping the Story on Track

The message of your story should be present from the beginning and become stronger as the story unfolds. Everything that happens throughout the story should build-up to the end, which is the most important part. You should describe in only a sentence or two what your audience should take away from the story, and build up to that as you craft the story. It is your job as the storyteller to guide your listeners/readers by unfolding the story to ensure that the message has an intended impact. Before beginning, you must have an understanding of what tone your message carries. Is this a funny story? A reality check? Is it intended to inspire the audience to be better people? Is it a vulnerable, emotional story that will make the audience think differently about something? It is your job to keep the tone of your message alive as you guide your readers/listeners through the story.

In the story of the grandfather who lost his best friend in World War II, for example, the importance of friendship is evident from the beginning. As your grandfather describes the experiences he had with his friend, both positive and negative, and their day-to-day life in the war, the theme of friendship prevails. You see both their happiest memories and the most significant challenges and the importance of their friendship in keeping each other going through the hardest times. The heart-shattering image of his friend being killed in battle and dying in his arms drives in the power of friendship, even in the moments of the most bitter loss. From here, it is clear to see how the power of friendship lives on, no matter what.

Defining your Goals

If the story is meant to be a reality check, you will want to provide your audience with an "I used to think this, but now I think this," moment. If your goal is to be funny, you'll need to ensure you have humor stitched throughout the plot, and you'll want to make sure the twist in the story is one that will make your audience laugh harder than they have in years. If the story is about morals, you will need to incorporate examples that cause the audience to think about moral decisions from a variety of perspectives and develop a strong sense of right and wrong within the context of the story. Keeping your listeners/readers engaged requires the use of dramatic tension and suspense to keep your audience on the edge of their seats, hardly able to stand the anticipation at what will happen next. No matter which direction you take with your story, you must clearly define the central theme.

Structure: Mapping it Out

When thinking about how to story structure, you should imagine your main message as the destination and the unfolding of the story as the destination. Each component of the structure can serve as a marker on the map to where you want your audience to end up. There are three large markers on the storytelling map: the inciting incident, rising action, climax, and resolution. Your navigation tools are 2 C's: Characters and conflict. These are the things that will keep your audience moving on their journey.

The starting place of your map is the character introduction and initial conflict. Regardless of who your characters are, you will need to introduce them quickly. Ensure the audience understands who each character is and what they mean to the story as you move into the actions. If you are the main character in your story, ensure that it is clear from the very beginning. It is important to provide great detail in your character descriptions.

Suppose the characters in your story have defining characteristics or elements of physical appearance, for example. In that case, a particular tattoo, style of dress, voice, or talent, this should be clear from the beginning. Establishing your characters in this way and building upon what makes them stand out will allow your audience to establish an immediate connection. To avoid overwhelming your audience and causing them to confuse characters, try to keep the number of characters in the story low.

If you are telling a personal story, there will likely only be a few central characters. If you are writing a story that is not based upon an event in your personal life, make sure you don't get carried away in the character planning. Try to stick to between three and five characters, and ensure that there is one central character.

Exploring the 2 C's: Character and Conflict

Your story's central character (whether it is yourself or someone else) should very quickly come into conflict with a force that challenges their character. Let's say, for example, that the character in your story is an exchange student traveling to a foreign country.

From the very beginning, you will want to clarify details about this person, such as where they come from, where they are going, and why. Perhaps they just graduated high school and felt the need to explore something new before starting college. The message of a story like this may be learning that love can overcome all boundaries and that the relationships people share are the most crucial thing with life. In this instance, let's imagine the story opens by putting the reader/listener in a moment with the exchange student on the plane, thinking about everything they are about to undertake. An example of an initial conflict that is on track with the story's message is the exchange student getting lost in an airport where hardly anyone speaks their language and begins to feel less confident and capable about their journey.

As the student attempts to navigate the airport, perhaps they also lose one of their bags or miss their flight. The student is likely feeling exhausted, defeated, and unsure of themselves and their journey. Be sure that as you introduce your characters and initial challenge, that you play into describing the surroundings. What time in history is it? What time of day? How can you describe the place this person is in and what emotions that setting invokes on them? Are they with other people or alone? The tension of this initial challenge is what will move the story forward towards the climax.

After this initial conflict, the rest of the story will likely deal with how the exchange student humbles themselves, learns the language of the country they are going to, and comes to understand the power of human interaction and relationships beyond language.

During this initial challenge to the main character, you should focus on inflicting tension and a sense of conflict that makes the reader think, connect, and wonder what will happen next. In the case of the exchange student story, imagine the story beginning, and ending, in the same airport, but with entirely different outcomes after the student has spent a year living abroad. If you are writing a funny story, consider building the humor up slowly, with small details that will make the final punchline all the more memorable.

Tying it All Together

Resolution is the next step after the climax has occurred. This is the part of the story that allows your audience to wind down and settle into the story's deeper meaning. This should be something that satisfies them and brings all of the story's other events full circle. In the case of the story with the exchange student, for example, we might see a resolution in which they are in the same airport they once got lost in, interacting freely with those around them and breathing in their last moments in that country, thinking of all their memories and how far they have come. These memories can serve as a callback to events that happened in earlier parts of the story and truly frame the audience's takeaway message.

Even in stories with a sad ending, such as the story of the grandfather's friendship with a fellow soldier killed in World War II, the audience will feel satisfied and inspired by the depth and power of friendship. Their hearts will be moved by the high emotionality of the story and the way that even though your grandfather's friend died much too soon, the power of their friendship could never die.

Assuming the Role of a Screenwriter

An excellent way to think about the structure of your story is to envision it as a movie. Imagine one of your favorite movies and how it unfolds to arrive at the screenwriter's message. Put yourself in the screenwriter's role and imagine a beginning, middle, and end of the story that will leave your reader feeling impacted and satisfied. It is crucial to carefully consider each of your story parts to avoid your audience becoming bored from the beginning, lost in the middle, or feeling completely dissatisfied at the end.

Chapter 2: Step 2 - Bringing the Audience In

The most compelling element of a good storyteller is the ability to keep the audience engaged from start to finish. To keep an audience engaged, you must first understand your audience. Different styles, lengths of stories, and messages will appeal to and be received by different groups. The story needs to be relevant to your audience. It is your job as the designer of the story to find points of interest that are specifically catered to your audience context and demographic. Whether your story is being presented to a classroom of Millennials, a business workplace, a group of elementary school-aged children, a group of Baby Boomers, or a particular religious group, you need to understand which styles of storytelling appeal to each of these groups, as well as what sort of attention span you can expect.

The tone to take with each of these groups varies greatly, and you can completely determine the impact of your story based upon how professional, friendly, vulnerable, approachable, fantastical, or down-to-earth your audience expects you to be.

Knowing your Audience

Your audience's understanding should determine which language you use to tell your story, which details will be most important to that audience, and how long you will take to write/tell the story. It is important never to assume that the audience knows everything you do. You need to do everything you can to avoid specialized language that will make people feel like outsiders and lose connection. This can include the use of abstract concepts or names that could cause more confusion than clarification from your audience.

In a dynamic, fast-paced workplace environment, or to a classroom of young people with short attention spans, you will not want your story to take longer than a few minutes to listen to or read through. At a specialized conference, however, your audience may be able to maintain engagement with a longer story. That being said, any story that drags on and on will eventually cause people's attention to wane. Some of the most meaningful stories are those which can unfold in a few words. Keep this in mind and try to make the story only as long as it needs to be to come full circle and leave the audience feeling satisfied.

Bridging the Gap

Once you have determined who your audience is, you must seek out where you can build a bridge between your characters and yourself. This story is yours, and you must establish a relationship between yourself and the audience.

Suppose you are speaking to an audience of college students, forever. In that case, you may establish a sense of relatability and "bridge the gap" by sharing a relevant story from when you were in college yourself. It is important to consider your relationship with the audience and what will make them feel connected to you and the story you have to share.

The bridge between your audience and your story goes two ways. To be fair to the audience, you must question your motivations in writing the story, and ensure that you will be able to approach it in a way that both speaks your message and keeps your listeners feeling connected.

Methods for Capturing Audience Attention

It is crucial to capture your audience's attention from the beginning of the story. One way to do this is by showing yourself or your main character (if it is not yourself) as someone likable. This can be established through humor or discussing a certain personal value.

Another way to establish audience engagement is by providing a point of connection between them and yourself or your main character through vulnerability. Sharing something personal and authentic is a great way to make your audience settle into the story and become invested in how things play out. There are comfort and appreciation provided by the vulnerability, and it has the power to set the tone for the rest of the story.

A final approach you may take in initial audience engagement is piquing their curiosity with a question, or by dropping them into an intense moment with little context. As your story unfolds, your mission is either to answer the question you posed, or provide context to the moment you described at the beginning. Suppose you begin your story with a question. In that case, you will ultimately be erasing any boundaries between your audience and your stories by making the audience feel that they are a central part of the story. If they feel that the narrative is unfolding around them, not outside of them, they are much more likely to stay engaged until the end and experience the unfolding of the story in a real, personal way.

Making your Audience Care

Regardless of which approach you to take; it is crucial to make your audience care. If the story starts too slow or begins to fall off track in the middle, your audience will lose interest and decide that they no longer care about what will happen next. This is especially true for people in today's fast-paced society. We live among people who gloss over texts and half-listen to others while thinking more about what they will say or do next. If it is not clear to you how your story is meaningful to a particular audience, it will certainly not be clear to the audience. To keep your audience presence throughout your story, they have to feel invested in the experience and see it as something that will benefit them somehow.

The WIIFM test stands for "What's in it for me." This is something your audience automatically wants to know. How can your story apply to their life? Will it inspire them? Open their mind? Teach them a new skill to make use of? Make them laugh, cry, or develop frustration which can fuel action?

Using the Power of Language

Another element of audience engagement is the use of vivid language and intonation. The power of language is universal, and you can use the tools of idiom, parables, and metaphors to inflict an emotional response from your audience. In the Biblical *parable of the Good Shepherd,* Jesus' love of his flock is symbolic of love for humanity as a whole. When one sheep wanders away from the flock, Jesus pursues that sheep until it has returned. The power of calling each sheep by name creates a feeling of personal connection and importance to the audience members.

Appealing to Audience Needs

When it comes to the art of storytelling, the audience's needs must be at the focus. This is a universal truth that surpasses cultural and traditional boundaries and contexts. Stories change slightly depending upon who it is being told to and where they're coming from. Good storytellers can meet their readers/listeners where they're at and focus upon what they seek and what will inspire them in the future.

Chapter 3: Step 3 - Making it Personal

A personal narrative is one of the most powerful tools you have at your disposal in the art of storytelling. This can take the form of telling a story that centers around you as the main character and an event that has occurred in your life. However, a personal narrative can also be infused into characters and scenarios you create. You can develop a mostly fictional story but maintains elements of your personal experience to keep the level of relatability alive. If there is one thing everyone can relate to, it is that we are all human beings with stories. It is vital to use elements of your own life to make waves in the art of storytelling.

If you choose not to tell your story from direct personal experience, the inspiration you draw from scenarios in your life can bring stories to life. Not only can this be a source of liberation in the way it allows you to bring elements of your experience to life in the way you see fit, but it is also crucial to storyteller/audience relations as well. In the example of the story of the friends from World War II, if you were choosing to write this story about your grandfather's experience, you would need to build that connection with him on a human level and determine how to relay that connection to your audience.

Making it Relatable

One of the most important things about sharing the personal narrative is the way it enhances the relatability factor between the storyteller and the audience. If your personal experience is tied into your story, the audience will be inspired to gain a deeper understanding of ultimately grows in empathy. The more people can empathize with the characters of a particular story, the more of an impact that story will have.

Let's consider you are telling a story to a class of college students regarding your own experiences in college. The goal of the story is to make them care about managing their time in college. A good way to keep them engaged is to start with a narrative they can relate to. For example, imagine you spent the night off campus one day and woke up late on the day of your first college exam. Not only are you late, but you also don't have the time to study for your exam that you had planned to take by waking up three hours beforehand to study. In the story, you leap from your bed frantically, throw on your clothes, and attempt to mumble what you could remember from your notes as you dashed out the door to your car.

On the way, you spill coffee all over your shirt. You are driving down the road, not paying attention, trying desperately to recall enough information to pass your first exam, when all of a sudden, you hear a horrible scraping noise on the side of your car. You look and see that you have hit one of the cars parked on the side of the street and that both of your mirrors have fallen off. At this point, you are twenty minutes late for your exam and have to email your professor and ask to go to his office to take it later. The message of this story is the importance of getting enough sleep and studying ahead of time, as well as not making decisions such as sleeping off campus the night before a big exam. By presenting an event that students can probably relate to some degree, your message will clearly come across.

Maintaining Balance of Details

An important thing to keep in mind if you are telling a true story is not to get carried away with details. If you include every single detail of the experience, it is much more likely that your audience will become lost and have difficulty distinguishing what is happening. This is another place where you must be critical and think about what your audience needs. Ask yourself which details are most crucial to the message of the story and which elements will be most likely to stick with your audience.

After determining the beginning and end of your story, dedicate your attention to the middle's details. Ensure that you provide enough detail to set the scene, but not so much that the message becomes muddled.

Writers Tip: Create a bulleted list of points in the plots which will occur between the beginning and end of your story. Check over the list several times, keeping in mind your message and the needs of the audience. Don't hesitate to add or take points off as needed.

Chapter 4: Step 4 - Creating an Emotional Experience

Think back to the last book you read, or film you watched, that seemed to take you beyond this realm of time and space and commanded your focus completely. If it was a book, perhaps it was one that you could not put down until the end, and if it was a movie, perhaps it was one that took you to an alternative reality and kept you on the edge of your seat with intensity. When it comes to your storytelling endeavors, you should strive to inflict these same feelings on your audience. This requires a great deal of attention to detail to ensure you create an atmosphere of intensity that will keep your audience emotionally involved. It is important to consider ahead of time which emotions you wish to play into. Should this story make your audience feel joyful? Inspired? Light-hearted? Melancholic?

Angry? Suspenseful? Take some time before you begin your story to narrow down the emotional experience you want the audience to have.

Setting the Scene

To capture your audience's senses and create an emotional experience, it is necessary to set a scene. Where is this story unfolding? What does the air smell like? What are the sights and sounds of the area? Keep in mind the time of year and the geographical location, as both of these things will inflict some sort of emotional response in your audience. If your audience feels immersed in the experience of a sea-side village, for example, they will be more likely to connect with the events that transpire there.

Embracing Conflict

It is crucial to embrace conflict as a storyteller—the conflict of the story is what will invoke the most emotions in your audience and keep them most heavily engaged. As you are crafting your narrative, consider each scene in depth. What obstacle does your main character (or yourself) face in each scene, and how do they overcome them? How should this obstacle make the audience feel? To achieve audience satisfaction when you reach the end of the story, you must cause them to experience the struggles of the main characters as they work to achieve their goals.

Examples of the Emotional Experience Scene 1

Let's go back to the story of the exchange student. In Scene 1, the audience is introduced to the character of the exchange student. They learn that she is from a small town in rural Nebraska, where she has lived for the entire eighteen years of her life. She is surrounded by people doing all the same things: graduating from high school, going to college or adopting a trade in the state, getting married, having kids, and staying in Nebraska until they die. She has always had a deep desire to see what the world has to offer outside of her small town, and she was thrilled when she stumbled across the opportunity to apply to be an exchange student. Now, she is finally on her way and is full of nervous excitement for all the unpredictability that she knows awaits her. This first scene invokes the emotion of excitement within your readers.

Examples of the Emotional Experience Scene 2

Now, let's move to Scene 2 of this story. In Scene 2, the exchange student has had two connecting flights and has landed at the airport of Sao Paulo, Brazil. This is her last stop before getting on her final flight to the city she will be staying in. Upon landing, she is unable to find her bags at the designated pick-up area and must embark on a nerve-wracking journey around the airport to find them. Because she can hardly speak Portuguese, and cannot find any attendants who speak English, she is faced with having to type phrases into Google Translate, holding them up to every attendant she sees and hoping they will be able to help her.

Meanwhile, she has no idea how to get to her next gate and has less than an hour before her flight will be taking off. As she runs around frantically, sleep-deprived, unable to communicate with those around her, and completely alone, the audience will have the same kind of tense, anxiety-ridden emotional experience that she is having. As the conflict mounts, the audience will be on the edge of their seats wondering if she will find her bags and get on the right flight, or if she will end up stuck in the airport trying to figure out what to do next.

Examples of the Emotional Experience Scene 3

In Scene 3, she stumbles upon her bags, which is a relief. However, after re-checking her bags, she has twenty minutes to get to her gate and no idea how to get there. She is going up and down escalators, running this way and that down the corridor, trying the same methods to speak with attendants, and nothing is working. Eventually, just as she has resigned herself to the reality that she will miss her flight, a young man about her age emerges from nowhere and comes up to her. He speaks in English, asking her "Are you lost?"

She learns that this boy is returning from a several weeks stay in New York, before which he was doing an exchange year in Ireland. He tells her he knew she was an exchange student because of her blazer and her lost expression. Shockingly, he reveals to her that they are going to the same city in Brazil and leads her to the correct gate. Before they board the plane, he gives her his phone number to reach out if she needs anything upon arrival. This young man becomes her best friend, and the core of her friend group in Brazil—he is the first person she meets within the circle of people who show her what love is, and how it can surpass all barriers. Of course, this moment fills the audience with emotions of relief and surprise at the irony of events.

Examples of the Emotional Experience Scene 4

In Scene 4, let's imagine the exchange student is back in the same airport one year later, after learning the Portuguese language and developing the closest relationships of her life with the young man she met at the airport, two other Brazilian women, and six exchange students from around the world who all lived in the same city. As she looks around at the surroundings, all the same as the last day she was there, and finds herself easily able to read the signs and converse with the attendants, she begins to cry tears of nostalgia and gratitude. She thinks to herself how this experience has been more than she ever could have asked for, and her heart feels broken in the best way possible from the kind of love she came to know while overseas. At this moment, the reader will feel satisfied as everything has come full circle and the student has reached her goals of finding a home in this foreign place. They will feel her pain in missing the people in whom she built her home, and their hearts will be full of the love she has come to know.

Bringing Joy to Yourself and the Audience

One of the most extraordinary things about storytelling about an experience that has meaning to you (whether it happened to you personally or not) is the joy it can bring to the storyteller. Through the art of storytelling, you can channel your personal emotional experience, adventures, and a message that is important to you, into a medium where they can live on forever. Perhaps the thing that makes storytelling most profound is how stories can be passed on from person to person, like gifts, and they bring joy to everyone who reads them. Stories have the power to light people's way into the future, and good stories never die.

Chapter 5: Step 5 - Writing the Unexpected

As human beings, we are full of stories. It is reasonable to claim that our lives are formed by the stories we hear (and remember) from others and the experiences we live, which become our own stories. Considering that we are flooded with thousands of stories throughout existence, it takes special work to make yours stand out. What will you do so that your readers will not only be impacted by your story but also will carry that impact with them into the rest of their lives?

Defying the Odds

To pull this off, you must be able to defy norms and go against the reader/listener's expectations to keep them engaged. Any element that works against your character's central desire is great to keep the reader engaged and keep the story moving forward. If you want your story to be one-of-a-kind, you have to write the unexpected. From the beginning of your story to the end, the audience should be faced with moment after moment that surprises them, makes them think differently, and overall keeps them in a state of awe. You may choose to take unusual directions in dialogue, setting, and characterization, and the best storytellers know how to use these things to give the story a memorable twist.

Developing your "Hook"

From the moment you begin your story, you have to be able to hook your reader. If you don't open the story in a way that strikes them, they will quickly lose interest and may stop paying attention.

There is no time in storytelling to "wait for it to get good"—it needs to be good from the start. It is essential to include an explosive moment in the introduction, which will grip your reader's heart, stir their emotions, and captivate their attention. Let's say, for example, you are writing a story that begins with a woman riding the bus into the city. From the beginning, you want to establish why she is riding the bus— perhaps she was recently in a car accident and has no vehicle.

You could begin the story by vaguely describing the setting, where she is going, and why she is on the bus. However, this narrative can become a lot more interesting and hook the audience if the story begins with a brief description of the setting, then the woman leans her head on her hand, closes her eyes, and begins to have flashbacks to a seizure she had while driving, which caused her car accident and thus, caused her to start taking the bus. This unexpected moment of the car accident flashback is much more intense. It gives the reader extra insight into the woman's life and a struggle she has already faced, which is more likely to keep the audience's attention.

Thinking Outside the Box with Conflict: Context, Flashback, Goals

When it comes to conflict, it would be easy to develop something like the woman getting caught in the rain or missing her bus. The problem with these conflicts is that they are to be expected when it comes to buses. To write the unexpected with your conflict, try to think outside the box. What other battles could this woman be facing?

Perhaps she takes the same bus every day to her job, and notices the same man on the bus almost every day, scribbling in his notebook. She is fascinated by how he appears and the energy he gives off, and she wants to talk to him. However, her mystery medical condition and potential for seizures drive her away from speaking to him, and she is too anxious to approach him. At this point, it is vital to provide some background information for context about her mystery illness, her uncertainty for her future, and perhaps how her illness impacted her last romantic relationship. This utilizes the flashback tool, which can provide the reader with more information and understanding of the depth of this character.

You could continue to write the unexpected by describing the complications the woman faces every day with her medical conditions, in more settings than simply on the bus. You could describe her lonely nights at home where she lives with her sister who is caring for her, her anxiety-ridden days at work, and endless trips to the hospital with no answers. Every day, the man on the bus is her ray of light, but she continues not to speak to him. At this point, talking to the man is her primary goal, with an overall goal of overcoming her fears, understanding her illness, and ultimately being able to love again.

Element of Surprise in the Climax

Now, let's imagine a scene where the man breaks the daily trend and asks if he can sit by her one morning on the bus. She obliges, they begin to talk, and then he invites her to coffee. They begin to form a relationship, but she keeps her guard up because she does not want to reveal her illness's secrets.

She tries to keep their interactions short, keep her sister on call, and enters every date with a silent prayer that she will not have a medical episode. This goes on until one night while they are having dinner at his apartment, she has a massive seizure and has to be taken to the hospital. This is the climax of the story, as her main goals come into question and her secret comes out.

Element of Surprise in the Falling Action and Resolution

To write the unexpected for this story's falling action, consider that the woman wakes up in the hospital to both her sister and the man beside her hospital bed. She breaks down and tells the man everything about her past, and how she does not know how anyone could love her under her condition, especially since there are so many unknowns. The man then reveals that he has such crippling social anxiety, he never believed he could approach a woman and talk to her, let alone find love. He admits to her that he is a poet and that every day they rode the bus together until he spoke to her, he had been writing poems for her. He had created a series in his journal called "The Woman on the Bus", in which he wrote down all the things he wished he could say to her but lacked the courage to. The man tells her that she has been his light, has given him space where he feels seen, and that he wants her no matter what. They both have health issues that seem invisible but impact them on a deep level, and they have found each other to work through those issues with. Once the woman gets out of the hospital, they continue together, loving each other and living their best lives. They both dedicate their time to creative ways to make people with disabilities, whether mental or physical, visible or invisible, feel seen, and deserving of love. This is an example of writing the unexpected in the resolution, as it takes the reader on a wild ride from hearing about a car accident and a mystery illness, to the conflict of falling in love and being too afraid to speak on it, to another conflict of keeping secrets as a romantic relationship deepens, to a scary medical incident, to a secret revealed about the other character, and finally, to an unexpected theme of love and the complexities of disability.

Brainstorming a Surprising Plot

If you are struggling to determine an adequately exciting plot, give yourself some time to brainstorm. Think of all of the sorts of things that could happen to your protagonist, and write them down. These events may be related to each other, but they do not have to be.

In this case, there were several exciting elements to the story.

1. The woman was struggling to be where she wanted to be in life

2. Had almost lost her life in a car accident

3. Had severe medical issues that no doctor could figure out

4. Had a tragic love story from her past relationship

5. Felt like her medical issues kept her from having the life she wanted

6. Fell in love with a man on the bus that she was too afraid to talk to

7. Eventually, he approached her

8. The two fell in love, but she was terrified to get too close

9. She ended up having a medical emergency and he figured out her secrets

10. He admits to her that he also has secrets regarding mental health issues that also make it hard for him to be where he wants in life

11. They end up pursuing a relationship together and changing the community by providing services to those with physical and mental illnesses/disabilities

Types of Conflict

Considering that conflict is one of the most critical elements of storytelling, it deserves a lot of attention when it comes to the prospect of writing the unexpected. As previously mentioned, conflict is the opposition that occurs between the character(s) and an internal or external force. Several ideas for potential disputes are as follows:

-Protagonist against nature: in which the protagonist faces challenges that arise from natural causes

-Protagonist against self: in which the protagonist is their most significant barrier to getting what they want, and they stand in their own way as a result of personal struggles and shortcomings.

-Protagonist against God: protagonist struggles against a sovereign force much greater than themselves, and their struggles seem practically inevitable and unavoidable.

-Protagonist against another individual: another character in the story does something that prohibits the protagonist from meeting their goal, and the protagonist must find a way to overcome it.

-Protagonist against society: the protagonist sees things differently or has different goals than the people around them, and no one seems to be on their side.

In the story idea, we see examples of the Protagonist against self as both characters battle with themselves on the journey of love.

Use of Progression

No matter what your conflict is, there are several things you need to keep in mind to keep your reader engaged and truly write something unexpected and memorable.

The first element of conflict to keep in mind is progression. Throughout the story, the protagonist's number and type of obstacles should be increasing and intensifying. In the story example, we see how the conflict goes from having to take the bus and being without a car, to having traumatic flashbacks, to living a life of doctor's appointments without answers and a life without direction, to the fear of love, to a medical emergency, and then to a plot twist moment of truth. This is an example of the progression of conflict in writing the unexpected.

Use of Mystery

Another critical aspect of the conflict is a mystery. It is essential to only explain things enough to give readers an idea, while still managing to keep them on the edge of their seats throughout the conflict. It is vital to avoid giving anything away before it is time. Along with that, it is crucial to maintain an element of surprise.

Keep things complex, engaging, and ready to go in any direction to keep the reader from being able to predict what happens next. By maintaining mystery and surprise elements, you are going against the audience's expectations and leaving them feeling more heavily impacted by what happened in the story.

Use of Empathy

Empathy also matters in writing the unexpected through conflict because it creates relationships between the characters and the audience. Often, the reader may be surprised by their connection with certain characters. They may find themselves rooting for someone they didn't expect to root for, or identifying with something they would never have imagined identifying with before. By creating this sense of empathy, the audience will find the characters' experiences resonating with them, whether in pleasant or unpleasant ways.

Use of Insight and Universality

Insight and universality are two other essential elements. The story should reveal something about human nature. In this story, there are several aspects of human nature revealed. The first is the idea surrounding struggle, and not being where you want to be in life.

The second is the deep and often terrifying experience of falling in love and letting another person see all of who you are. However, at the end of the day, this story demonstrates that the power of love, honesty, and compassion is more significant than any obstacle. In terms of universality, this story presents struggles that most readers, from most cultures, backgrounds, etc. will resonate with, simply because they are human. No matter where you are, what beliefs you hold, or what your personal experience has been, everyone can understand the power and complication of love, how it feels to be afraid, and what it is like to be kicked by life when you're down. People will care about this story because they care about love, about facing fears, and about being able to find purpose in life.

Creating a High Stakes Environment

Lastly, it is vital to create a high stakes environment surrounding the story's conflict. To keep the audience engaged, they must know that the story matters. There has to be something at stake—something precious that could be lost. To write the unexpected, consider what is at stake and the unique difficulties that pose a threat to that thing.

Experimenting with Point of View

One tip to apply to the process of writing the unexpected is to experiment with a variety of points of view. You can maintain an element of surprise and interest by writing the story in a unique style or from a voice the audience wouldn't expect. Once you have written your story, try out the effects of various points of view. Just remember, do not give the narration to a nonessential character. The storyline must revolve around a character who is central to the action, to avoid audience confusion.

Chapter 6: Step 6 - Build up to a Positive Outcome

The most important part of storytelling is the feelings you invoke in your audience at the end. As a storyteller, it is your job to bring things full circle and make it clear to the audience why everything happened the way it did and the more profound message of the story. If you leave the audience hanging and unable to identify the point, they will feel a sense of dissatisfaction with the story as a whole. One crucial part of the storytelling process is building up the sequence of events to a positive outcome.

Bringing the Story Full Circle

In both of the story ideas we discussed previously in this guide, we saw how the events the characters experienced led them to a happy and satisfying ending. The exchange student endured the difficulties of doubting her decisions and feeling lost and alone. Still, over time her experience built her into someone who not only had new language skills and cultural understanding but also an understanding of humanity itself on a deeper level and the strength of connections among humans.

In the woman's story on the bus, several things are happening that make her life extremely difficult. The reader may be left to wonder if she will ever find love or fulfillment, or if she will even be able to survive for long with her invisible medical condition. Will she ever get a diagnosis? Will this illness end up claiming her life entirely? At the end of the story, there is a resolution in the case of the woman finding love and the connection she makes with another person who has struggled with succeeding in society and feeling deserving of love. Although it is not clear if the woman will live a long life, the audience is provided with the positive outcome of the relationship between the man and the woman, the life they begin to build together, and how they help other people based upon their experiences.

Tying Positive Outcome to Emotional Experience

Although both of these stories have relatively "happy endings", a positive outcome does not always have to be happy. Consider, for example, the last time someone told you about an incredibly sad film, but also exceptionally good. Some of the best stories have endings in which somebody dies, the couple doesn't end up together, etc. but if these stories are told right, they speak to live and create a deeper sense of awareness within the audience. These endings can be even better than "happy endings", because life is a never-ending cycle of conflict, resolution, and learning experiences, and "happy endings" do not truly exist on a human level. The ending can make the reader feel sad, angry, or solemn, and individual audience members may even decide that they hate the story. However, as long as there is a profound emotional impact, and the audience can somewhat understand why things happened the way they did (even if they wished for a different result), the storyteller has done their job of building up to a positive outcome.

Brainstorming Outcome Possibilities

One tip to try out in developing your positive outcome is brainstorming all of the outcome possibilities. Think of various emotions: happy, sad, angry, fearful, hopeful, surprised, confused, etc. Then, assign different endings to the story based upon each emotion. Consider everything that leads up to the outcome, and ask yourself which end has the most significant emotional impact on you. If you can't decide, consider presenting your ideas to a trusted individual who can tell you which end has the largest emotional impact on them. To try this out, let's reconsider the story of the couple who met on the bus, assigning different endings based upon each emotion we encounter.

Happy Ending

The man reads the love poems he wrote about the woman every day as she recovers in the hospital, and she listens and learns from him about how social anxiety has impacted his life. The two begin to brainstorm ways to shed light on individuals fighting physical and mental battles that are not evident from the outside. Soon after the woman is released from the hospital, they move in together, get married, and start a project called "Letters from the Invisible." In this project, they have people all over the world write letters about why they feel invisible, specifically concerning disabilities. They respond and help develop policies that are more inclusive and aware of the struggles people face.

Sad Ending

The woman reveals her condition to the man before she has her medical episode, and she breaks up with him. He does not yet reveal to her how much he loves her, or how hard it was for him to approach her, nor does he tell her about the letters he wrote. He begs her to stay, but she doesn't, convincing him it is for his good. When she has her medical emergency, her sister calls him, and he rushes to the hospital to be by her side. When she wakes up, she can't speak, but he tells her everything that he had been too afraid to share. He reads the letters to her every day and does not leave her side. On the day he tells her he loves her; she squeezes his hand three times in response. A few hours later, she dies. Although this ending is heartbreaking, there is still a sense of positive outcome because there is nothing left unexpressed, and the depth of true love rings true.

Angry Ending

The woman finally finds the courage to reveal to the man what she has been going through on her medical journey. As much as he tries to be there for her, he can't find it within himself to be able to support her, primarily because of everything he is dealing with on a psychological level. He ends up ending the relationship, at which point the audience will be angry with him and very concerned about her well-being. At this point, out of defiance, she discovers the importance of self-love and begins writing poetry about what it is like to live with an invisible illness and overcome the daily obstacles, especially as it pertains to love. She establishes a future for herself and becomes successful. The anger of him ending the relationship leads to clarity on her end, and she discovers something crucial about herself and her journey. Although the reader may feel angry at the situation, there is still a positive outcome in the message of self-love, independence, and overcoming obstacles.

Fearful Ending

After the woman's medical emergency, she and the man grow together, tell each other their stories, move in together, get married, and take all the other steps of the happy ending. However, in the fearful ending, perhaps the man's psychological health continues to worsen as the couple grows older, until he reaches a point where it is too difficult for him to talk, function, or live out his dreams with his wife.

Additionally, he may be unable to support her, and the task of defending him falls on her shoulders, even though she is still chronically ill, and they have grown older. Perhaps he eventually has to go into a care facility and loses recollection of who she is altogether. She has to move back in with her sister, and when she comes to visit him, he doesn't recognize her but achieves peace when she reads him the old letters he wrote her about "The Woman on the Bus." This ending may inflict fear in the audience because it shows how even when things seem happy at first, life is impermanent and there is always the risk of bad things happening and not going as planned. However, it also provides a solemn dose of reality, leading them to be more attentive and grateful in daily life.

Hopeful Ending

After the hopeful ending, the doctors tell the woman that they do not know how to figure out what is going on with her. She stops doing frequent doctor's visits and chooses simply to live in the moment with her love, making a difference in the world, and not being held back by her illness. Although it is unclear how long she will live, the audience can be filled with hope as she chases her dreams and pursues the fullest life possible despite the circumstances. This ending is more ambiguous and provides the reader with a sense of hope that the woman will survive, the couple will grow, and the world will continue to be changed by their legacy.

Surprising Ending

The woman wakes up after her medical emergency and has a realization about what she truly wants. She begins to understand that the thing she is truly looking for in life is the love she can provide to herself and how she can use her story to inspire other people. Although the man professes his love to her, she denies him, wishing him the best and telling him that they both should spend their time focusing on how to make others feel seen and recognize that the greatest kind of love is self-love.

They maintain a friendly relationship, but both pursue individual paths which are not focused on romance, but instead on self-healing and healing the world. This ending may also inflict feelings of anger in the reader, but ultimately, it is still a positive outcome that holds a more profound message and ties all previous events together.

Confusing Ending

An example of a well-done confusing ending would be one in which, after the woman's medical emergency, the couple takes the risk to move in together. They have no idea what they will do next or if either of them will live beyond the next day, but they choose to surrender to that and focus on being together. This ending may leave the reader feeling confused, wondering if either of them ever receives a diagnosis, if they die, or if they continue to struggle in society. It is important to address confusing endings with caution. Having a confusing end, and leaving the audience feeling lost as a result of an incohesive series of events, are two very different things.

Confusing endings are built up to by a sequence of logical events that lead to an open-ended outcome. This type of outcome is positive because it allows the audience to take the events of the story and what they know of the characters and draw their conclusions about what may have happened. This is a profoundly intellectual experience that requires an understanding of the story's primary message(s) and is sure to leave a long-term impact on the reader as they consider all the possibilities of what may have happened to the characters.

Chapter 7: Step 7 - Developing a Shining Moment

To share a great story is to give your audience a gift that can last them a lifetime. In many ways, storytelling is the gift that keeps on giving because it can be passed from person to person, continuing to form generations of people long after it is first told. Since the beginning of humankind, stories have been shaping reality as we know it and drastically changing the world's course and the ways we understand each other. As a storyteller, you have a major role to play in this process of bestowing gifts on humanity. Throughout this guide, we have explored many of the methods of developing top tier storytelling skills. In this final chapter, we will discuss one final element that is crucial to the storytelling process—developing a shining moment.

Central Character Dilemmas

No matter what your story's content is, or what main message you choose to express, your characters will be faced with conflict as the story unfolds. There will be times when your characters will be faced with difficult decisions, and sometimes, they may make the wrong decision. This not only creates a moral complication within the story and deepens the emotional experience, but it also creates a sense of integrity and sets expectations for the characters to live up to. Oftentimes, when a central character is faced with a difficult decision, they may choose the "wrong" option and be de-railed as they have to come to terms with their mistake and fix it.

Creating a Growth Experience

Your storytelling process should be like a rollercoaster ride in which your readers are emotionally invested and hanging on tight for what comes next. It is your job as the storyteller to take them on the journey with the characters. As your characters continue to grow and learn the lessons which are central to the theme of the story, your audience will learn and grow as well. Give them moments to root for the character, to hurt for them, and perhaps to feel angry or annoyed at them for making the "wrong" decisions. From here, you can build up to the "make it or break it" element of your story—the shining moment.

Creating Shining Moments that Stick

The shining moments are the things that tend to stick with us most about the stories we hear. Does your central character lead an army to victory after a vicious war? Do they learn the art of self-love after years of searching for romance? Do they die for a worthy cause? Do they recover from a history of addiction and pursue work in the field of providing help to other addicts? No matter what the shining moment is, it must be in direct alignment with the story's theme. The shining moment you determine for your character may vary depending on what you hope the audience will take away. For this reason, it is a good idea to play with ideas for shining moments in the same way you play with positive outcomes/endings. The decisions you make on these areas will shape the track of your entire story, and therefore, should be roughly developed before you get too far into the writing process itself.

Combining Shining Moment with Positive Outcome

The decisions you make about your shining moment go hand-in-hand with the idea of a positive outcome, as described in Chapter 6. Once you have determined the general emotional experience to take with your positive outcome, you can identify your shining moment within it. Let's take a look at the examples of each kind of outcome discussed in Chapter 6 for the story of the couple who met on the bus, and consider how the shining moments could vary for each one.

Happy Ending Shining Moment

In this example of a positive outcome, the shining moment is focused on both central characters. First of all, the man experiences a shining moment by overcoming his anxiety enough to tell the woman how he feels, sharing his deepest vulnerabilities with her through reading the letters. The two then experience a shining moment as a couple as they take everything that has happened to them and begin to develop a plan to help other people who have felt beaten down or unseen by society.

As they build a life together and create the legendary project "Letters from the Invisible," everything comes full circle. It leaves the audience feeling proud and inspired by the theme of the story and the way the characters have reacted in response to the difficulties they have faced.

Sad Ending Shining Moment

In this ending, the man still has a shining moment when he rushes to the hospital to be there for the woman even after she has broken up with him. He sets himself and his fears aside and does not leave her side, while also opening himself up to be vulnerable with her and share his heart through the reading of the letters. He demonstrates his shining moment by the acts of love shown while she is in the hospital and by eventually swallowing his fear to a point where he can finally tell her the truth—that he loves her. She joins in the shining moment at this point when she squeezes his hand three times to signify her love so that even once she has died the audience can walk away knowing that nothing was left unsaid.

Angry Ending Shining Moment

In this ending, the woman is the one with the most prominent shining moment, as she overcomes the challenge of being left after revealing the truth to the man about her medical journey. Although she is in pain, she makes the most of it, pursuing her dreams with all she has and making a change in the world on her own. She discovers self-love and begins to express herself creatively in a way that has incredible success. She speaks her truth about living with an invisible illness and how she overcame the obstacles she faced and learned how to adore herself and pave the way to her future. In this example, her clarity and self-discovery are the shining moments of the story.

Fearful Ending Shining Moment

In this ending, the man's shining moment of caring for and expressing his vulnerabilities to his wife while she was sick transitions into the woman's shining moment, of doing the same for him after he has begun to go downhill psychologically. Even though he can no longer support her in the way he once did, and she has to face the challenges of having him forget who she is and moving back in with her sister, she exhibits extreme dedication, support, and unconditional love on her visits when she reads him the letters from the past. Despite the incredibly difficult and scary circumstances, her strength prevails, and she manages to find gratitude and bring peace to her love every single day. This gives us a shining moment in which, even amid trial, heartbreak, and the fear of life's impermanence, love trumps all.

Hopeful Ending Shining Moment

With this ending, the shining moment is the woman choosing to live in defiance of her circumstances, choosing joy, gratitude, and the fullest life possible despite her mystery medical journey. She decides to place more of her energy in day-to-day life and how she can make the world a better place, as opposed to allowing uncertainty about her health and the future to hold her back. Her shining moment is, despite her life circumstances, living life to the fullest and understanding what the meaning of life is truly all about

Surprising Ending Shining Moment

In this ending, the woman once again is the character who experiences the larger shining moment. After her last medical emergency, she makes a powerful realization about what she is truly searching for in life, and that is the love that only she can provide for herself, and the legacy she can create by sharing her story in the world. She makes the bold decision to tell the man they should go their separate ways and pour their energy into building individual legacies, and that is precisely what happens. At this point, the shining moment ends with both of them on a journey of self-healing and changing the world.

Confusing Ending Shining Moment

The shining moment in this ending happens as the couple decides to take the leap and move in together. They surrender to their life exactly as it is and choose to make the best of it for as much time as they have left. During this time, the couple continues to grow in love with one another and realizes that daily life is a gift, and our presence in each moment is crucial.

Leaving Space for Evolution

What if you think you know what your shining moment will be, but as you develop the story, you find it takes on a mind of its own? If this happens, don't be alarmed. Although it is important to have a vague idea of what the shining moment will be to keep yourself on task and prevent audience boredom or confusion, it is certainly okay to adhere to the way the story changes after you have started writing. Give yourself the freedom to make adaptations as you go—just remember to keep revising to make sure you're still on track.

Conclusion

When you started this guide, you knew that storytelling was a universal talent—one which you desired to grow your skills in. Throughout the guide, you were provided with the ins and outs of storytelling, things to avoid, and tips to apply to keep yourself on track, keep your audience engaged, and arrive at a legendary shining moment. As you learned these methods, you also discovered the fact that storytelling is one of the greatest gifts you can give. Once you have gifted your audience with a good story, they may take it forward. Now that you understand the power held by storytellers, and how to exhibit that power, you have everything you need to be on your way.

You began this journey by uncovering the purpose of the story being told and how to organize and structure it. You discovered the importance of the 2 C's, character development, clarifying primary goals, and tying everything together throughout the story. Next, you learned methods of engaging your audience and keeping their attention throughout. You discovered the importance of storytelling as an emotional experience and how you can use personal narrative to achieve this and make your readers feel it. The guide went on to implement strategies for maintaining an element of surprise. You learned the importance of bringing things full circle with a positive outcome and creating a shining moment for the audience to take with them and continue to share — keeping your story alive for years to come.

Book 3: How to Edit Writing

7 Easy Steps to Master Writing Editing, Proofreading, Copy Editing, Spelling, Grammar & Punctuation

Jaiden Pemton

Introduction

When it comes to editing, it is crucial to take your time and be thorough, give attention to the seemingly minor details, and interact with the material on a deeper level to ensure the purpose is being fulfilled. No matter which industry you're working with in the writing world, editing is a universal requirement. Whether you're editing your own writing or serving as an editor for another writer, this guide will show you the top-notch editing strategies, which will be sure to set the content you edit apart in your industry and yield ultimate success as an editor.

It is not possible to predict exactly how many drafts you will need to generate before a piece of writing is ready to go out into the world. Ultimately, the more thorough you are, the fewer drafts you will need to generate. The task of editing requires deep focus and willingness to engage with the content wholly to catch the smallest mistakes, inconsistencies, or areas where the text's purpose is getting lost. Whether you are editing your own writing or someone else's, it is crucial to develop skills that set you apart and help you achieve the most accurate and efficient editing strategy.

When it comes to editing, it is easy to fall into the trap of getting bored or exhausted by the content and skimming over important details. You may reach a point where you have looked over the same words so often. You struggle to determine the right word to use when something doesn't sound right or figuring out how to re-instate the purpose.

You may find yourself feeling so eager to have the content wrapped up and turned in that you start missing small details, which can be a vital mistake. As the editor, it is your job to get the piece of writing that is as close to perfection as possible. If your text is full of errors you did not catch in the editing stage, it will push readers away. This guide will provide you with ideas for maintaining your own energy and enthusiasm throughout the editing process and utilizing tactics such as giving the writing space and editing in reverse to keep a fresh perspective.

In this guide you will find a comprehensive step-by-step reference format with everything you need to know about the editing process. You will be provided with in-depth knowledge of the stages of editing, the importance of reading work aloud, how to manage the small formatting details, how to deeply interact with the content to ensure the message is getting across, and creative strategies you can implement to look at the content differently. Additionally, the guide contains excellent tips for keeping your editing process lively and engaged the whole way through.

The chapters of this guide will take you through each step of the editing journey to help you avoid common mistakes and develop your own thorough process. Each chapter is designed with astounding detail to help you stay on track and address any questions or concerns you have along the way.

Chapters are subtitled and easy-to-follow with examples of tips, tricks, techniques, and things to avoid. Regardless of if you are editing your own writing or someone else's, this guide has all the tools you need to set yourself apart as an expert editor and is sure to serve as the perfect guide to revolutionize your editing experience.

Happy writing!

Chapter 1: Step 1 - Breaking Editing into Stages

As an editor, your role is to make sure everything is clear to the reader. If the reader struggles to read the text, either because it is swaying from the purpose or there are too many mistakes with formatting or grammar, they will have a much harder time reaching the end of the piece. Your job is to advocate for the reader by making their journey through the text as easy as possible and ensuring that they are impacted by the text when they reach the end. To increase levels of clarity and consistency for the reader, you must be persistent in the correction and improvement process. Your role as the editor includes correcting the structure, style, grammar, spelling, punctuation, point of view, and information order. Before you begin, it is vital to familiarize yourself with the client's guidelines (if you are editing for another writer) or the publisher.

Breaking Down the Stages

The editing process includes several stages. The first stage is structural or developmental editing, in which you complete a rough copy edit. Line editing and copy editing are the second stages of the process, and the rough copy edit is the result of this stage. The final step is the fine or final copy edit, which involves final proofreading and preparing for the graphic design and "final proof" stages, which will occur right before publication.

In some cases, if the writer has already done a great deal of initial self-editing on the piece, the structural stage may not be necessary, as the work is already structurally sound. If you are writing and editing your own piece, you will need to make plans to send it on to a professional editor to ensure the work is structurally sound, and then again for the final proofreading. This is because, at some point, you will have been looking at your content so much that you will not be able to target any other edits that need to be made.

Stage 1: Structural Editing

The role of the structural editor is to review the writing from a broader standpoint. The structural stage is not meticulously examining the details but instead considering the text's more significant picture issues. This editor needs to be aware of who the target audience is and the author's primary goal. Editors of fiction stories need to ensure that the plot, dialogue, character, and point of view are clearly expressed and follow the same structure. Editors of nonfiction should examination the general organization of the content and question it for clarity and consistency of the argument and supporting evidence.

Scheduling Structuring Consultations

Suppose the structural editor is not the writer of the manuscript. In that case, they will need to consult with the author to discuss the main idea the author is trying to express so they can evaluate it for clarity. Additionally, the author and structural editor should confirm the style manual that is expected in editing. They should be on the same page regarding the style which will be used, which can be defined in a style sheet. The style sheet is a tool for the structural editor to refer back to throughout the editing process, including all necessary rules regarding punctuation, fonts, headings, capitalization, etc.

Once the editor has come up with a list of structural edits, they will need to meet with the author again to discuss the structural improvements and why they are suggesting them. The structural editor may find that the manuscript is structurally sound and does not need many modifications and, therefore, may advise the author to proceed to the copyediting stage.

Determining the Authority of the Structural Editor

In some cases, the structural editor and the author may agree that the structural editor has full flexibility with their changes, including length, word count, number of chapters, or even the point of view. However, in other cases, the structural editor may be expected to consult with the author to receive approval before making any corrections. Another option is for the structural editor to make all corrections as suggestions in a separate draft and submit it to the client so that all the edits made are visible and can be approved or declined.

Increasing Clarity and Consistency

The structural editor must keep in mind that their job is not to entirely change the manuscript but rather, to make it better. That said, they should move and delete sentences or paragraphs only when it is altogether necessary to increase clarity and consistency. The structural editor can make suggestions on switching the order of chapters, creating new chapter sections, adjusting the table of contents, or creating appendices, descriptions, or introductions.

Focusing on the Bigger Picture

Although the structural editor can correct grammar, spelling, and punctuation, this is not their primary focus. The manuscript will endure further stages of editing, which are more dedicated to these small details. The structural editor should maintain focus on the bigger picture. They should be asking themselves if the way the text is set up is easy to follow, if the theme is being clearly expressed throughout the manuscript etc. If the structural editor is different than the editors who will be working on the manuscript in its later stages, they may choose not to correct the finer details.

Stage 2: Line Editing

The first part of copy editing (the second stage of the editing process) is line editing. The line edit is sometimes called a "rough copy edit" and can only occur after the manuscript has been evaluated for structural soundness. The line editing process does not aim to correct every minor error but rather to continue building on the manuscript's consistency as a whole. The copy editor will check for ways to improve the tone and style to better match the manuscript's goals. If fact-checking needs to occur, the line editing phase is where that will happen. The line reader should fact check information such as places, links, events, and references provided in the manuscript to ensure that the statements are correct. If the manuscript needs an index, it will require a separate "editing pass," which can be done by an indexer or by the line editor.

Addressing Structural Inconsistencies

The role of the line editor is to catch any structural issues which may have been overlooked. If there are remaining structural errors, the manuscript may require further structural editing. The line editor must bear in mind the manual guide chosen for the document to ensure that all of the content is per this manual. The line editor will rely on the style sheet to ensure consistency and add to the style sheet. The style sheet serves as an outline for rules concerning punctuation, spelling, acronyms, capitalization, fonts, and heading and is crucial for creating dependability within the manuscript.

Catching Major Spelling, Punctuation, and Grammatical Errors

As the line editor proceeds through the editing process, they have the authority to make grammatical changes, move sentences and paragraphs around, select deletion of repetitive information, and suggest rewrites for sentences and paragraphs. Their goal is to catch the significant spelling and punctuation errors to improve the grammar of the manuscript.

Conducting Editing Passes

In many cases, the manuscript will pass through a variety of line editing stages. Each stage is considered an 'editing pass,' Each manuscript requires a different number of passes to ensure that all significant corrections have been made. The line editor's role does not extend to correcting minor errors; however, more minor errors may be encountered as the manuscript goes through more passes.

Creating the Final Copy Edit

The final stage of the copyediting process is the most meticulous of all. It is the final stage of corrections before the final design and proofreading stages before publication. If the writing will not be published, the 'final copy edit' is the final stage of the editing process. The stakes are high in this stage, and the process is more detailed.

When copyediting things like newsletters, applications, and reports, which are not going to be published, the copy editor can assume that the document has already undergone self-editing and should not address too many errors. The copy editor strives to catch the last remaining grammatical, punctuation, or spelling errors that were not detected during the initial editing stages.

In the case of a manuscript that will be published, it must receive a final copy edit before it is sent into the final stages of design and proofreading before publication. Manuscripts that need this last copy edit before the designing stage are fiction or nonfiction manuscripts, annual reports, or any other report that will be distributed publicly.

Checking the Manuscript with Fresh Eyes

The copy editor's role is to catch any basic editing that was missed in the line editing stage, using the style sheet and any other manual guides for reference on appropriate stylistic decisions. With fresh eyes, the copy editor will correct any minor mistakes that have not previously been addressed. They will check for any inconsistencies in the text and deal with information such as appendices, index, publication information, and the table of contents that have not been addressed by the line editor.

Preparing for the Final Stage

After the first copy editing pass occurs, the copy editor will work with the author to determine if it is sufficient or needs to go through another pass to ensure no errors. Before the document is turned in or passed on to the design stage, the copy editor must be able to confirm with confidence that there are no errors, and the document is fully ready for the following step.

Chapter 2: Step 2 - Reading Work Aloud

Have you ever been trying to edit an essay with a peer or teacher and been told to "Try reading it aloud?" This is a common editing strategy because it pulls us out of the space of skimming and forces us to engage with the text differently. The process of reading aloud can serve as a useful tool to catch the areas that seem "off" but can be easily ignored when reading the text in your head.

Reading aloud not only builds continuity and confidence with what has been written, but it also helps you to engage with the meaning differently, comprehend what is on the paper, identifying the writing voice, and establishing areas where the flow could be improved.

Significant Benefits of Reading Aloud

There are several significant benefits to reading aloud. The first is that the process of reading aloud helps you to hone in on dialogue and narrative, capture its real authenticity, and ensure that all the right characters are speaking at the right time to keep things flowing. Reading aloud is visual and helps paint a picture in your mind as you read the text, leading you to make changes or say more in some text regions to make these images more potent for the reader.

Reading aloud also yields a more remarkable ability for self-expression. If you are the writer and the editor of your own piece, reading aloud can help establish the connection between your speaking and writing voice. Additionally, reading aloud helps build on your internal listening skills, which can help you tune in to the writing voice of yourself (if you are editing your own work) or the writer you are working for. This can yield more significant success in future writings.

Editing for Clarity and Correctness

In terms of editing for clarity and correctness, reading aloud helps you to sound out words, catch stumbling blocks created by poor punctuation, detect the use of syllables, and catch misspellings. It is much easier to tell if a sentence is a run-on or a word is misspelled if you have the chance to verbalize it. Not only is reading aloud the best way to establish fluidity, build connections, and catch otherwise unnoticeable errors in the text you edit, it can also develop your skills in public speaking.

Reading Aloud as a First Step

When it comes to editing your writing, reading aloud is crucial in catching the mistakes that become easy to miss. As soon as you finish writing your piece, it's a good idea to read it aloud before doing anything else. This is an excellent tactic for catching some initial structural and grammatical errors right from the beginning, which will make the rest of the process much more comfortable. As you read the writing aloud, keep a pen or highlighter handy that you can use to mark areas where you notice yourself stumbling or feeling confused at what was just said.

Establishing Text Flow

When you read aloud, you can establish how your writing flows, how a particular section works (or doesn't work) with the next, and if you are staying in the active voice. One of the best ways to catch passivity is through the reading aloud process. If you find yourself stumbling or getting lost on the message of what you're reading, that is a clear sign that edits are needed.

As you read your work aloud, it becomes clearer whether or not the correct punctuation marks are being used. If you notice pauses, questions, or exclamations in your oral reading, there is reason to believe you should either insert a comma or add a period. If you find yourself going on and on in a single sentence, that's a good sign that sentence is a run-on and needs to be broken up. By listening to your pauses, you can better avoid punctuation errors and run-on sentences. The read-aloud also gives you a process to question your grammar and the meaning of the work. If you don't know what you're reading about, your other readers certainly will not.

Deepening Reader Understanding

To that same token, if you find yourself growing bored as you read, it's a good sign that a particular section needs to be cut.

Boredom while reading is usually a result of the momentum slowing down too much or the writing theme becoming lost to leave the reader asking, "What's going on here and what's the point?" If you feel like a specific section of the writing is slow or confusing, it should either be changed or cut out entirely.

Verbalizing as a Thinking Tool

Saying things out loud about your writing can also be helpful when it comes to remembering ideas for later. If you have an idea but can't write it down, speak it into existence. Listening to yourself talk about it can help form the idea into a memory that you can later take back to your writing desk. Similarly, as you come up with new ideas of things to write or elements to add to your pieces, talk the ideas through with yourself beforehand. It's a good idea to speak these ideas out loud, ask yourself questions the reader may ask, work through inconsistencies and unclear parts, and genuinely engage with the dialogue. In doing this, you can already bring an outside voice to your writing, which can help eliminate ideas that won't get you very far and encourage you to think more.

Personifying Dialogue

Because dialogue is a verbal exchange between multiple characters, the only way to truly measure its efficiency is by verbalizing it. One way to do this is by viewing the dialogue like that of a script. As you read, pay attention to how natural and authentic the dialogue sounds. Does it sound rigid or overly rehearsed? Is each line being spoken necessary? Is there more that needs to be said? Does the correct character talk about each line, or should someone else be saying it? To keep your readers engaged, you must establish this sense of engagement in yourself by reading aloud.

Making Pace Adjustments

Reading your work aloud helps with pacing as it gives you an idea of which parts of the writing are fast-pasted and engaging and where things slow down. Once you have this knowledge, you can question whether or not certain areas are moving too quickly and trying to tackle too much (which can leave the reader feeling confused and strung along) or if they are too slow (which can leave the reader feeling bored and uninspired).

Using your pen or highlighting tool, mark the areas where you notice significant differences in the pacing, and ask yourself if each scene is correctly paced or would be more potent if it was slowed down or sped up. Slowing things down can help the reader take a break from something hectic that just happened or build tension for something wild that is about to happen. Reading aloud is the only way to catch these pacing details.

Honing in on Important Details

Along with improving your pacing, reading aloud also serves to enhance the flow of the writing. As mentioned previously, it is easy for our brains to skip over the seemingly minute details to get to the point of what we are reading. This is especially true if you have been looking at the same piece of writing repeatedly. At some point, your subconscious begins to ignore the finer details. Eventually, even as you read aloud, you may find yourself trying to skip words or move things around. Make a note of these things and ask yourself if your natural desire to do this warrants some sort of change in the text.

Establishing Specific Areas to Edit

Hearing the work you have written read aloud often brings things to light that are hard to notice as our eyes repeatedly scan the page. In the early editing stages specifically, there is a lot more work to be done than we may realize. The writing may be too wordy, too fast, too slow, or lack emotion and passion, have inefficient dialogue, or simply lack interest level. If you are a writer who plans to send your manuscript to an editor to work with, be sure to read it aloud and sort through things first. This way, you can provide more input to your editor on what you need help with. If you are the editor of someone else's work, encourage them to read it aloud beforehand so they can provide more of a basis for discussion. Once it is in your hands, continue to read it aloud until everything sounds right.

Reading Aloud to Others

The final step of reading work aloud in the editing process is to read aloud to another person (or people). The person you read in front of can be anyone from a close friend, family member, or partner, to a peer or even a stranger. Regardless of who you choose to read aloud to, you can rely on the innate appreciation of social behavior to increase your desire to solve problems and pay more in-depth attention to the writing.

Reading aloud is typically a more vulnerable and intimidating experience, especially if you read something you wrote yourself. When we read material aloud, our natural social instincts become heightened because we know other people listen to us and draw opinions from what we say. We have an innate desire to perform well in front of others and receive positive feedback. Your responses will be heightened from this space of vulnerability and slight nervousness, and you may notice things you began to ignore in previous readings subconsciously. You will be extra sensitive to inconsistencies in pace, rhythm, and flow, as well as if a particular section drones on for too long. This heightened sensitivity will allow you to make even more changes and come closer to perfection than you could be reading only to yourself. In this state, you will also have a deeper appreciation for the writing structure, and your desire to produce a pleasing effect will increase.

The heightened sensitivity and social pressure of reading aloud to another person will make the errors in grammar, flow, and punctuation leap out even further, as you will feel nervous about making mistakes. You will be likely to look upon the writing with more meticulous eyes as you consider the fact that other listeners are drawing their conclusions and making their judgments. This will motivate you to solve the problems you encounter within the text as quickly and efficiently as possible.

Chapter 3: Step 3 - Setting Things Apart

When it comes to elements like headings, captions, indexes, appendixes, tables, and contents lists, it can be hard to stay focused. Writers tend to focus more on the main point of what they are trying to say, the characters they develop, and what they want the reader to take away. It is typical for the seemingly fewer essential elements of the writing to slip through the cracks. With the competition of the writing industry and the bustling state of the world, editors cannot afford to be careless with these elements.

Giving Readers Something to Skim

As people navigate their busy lives, they are more likely to skim through writing than profoundly engaging from start to finish. To capture the reader's attention, you must be concise and convincing, drawing them to slow down and engage more deeply with what is being said. When a customer is looking for a piece of content to contend with, they are not reading page after page of the writing itself. Instead, they are looking at the headings, captions, indexes, appendixes, tables, and contents lists to tell them more about what to expect and help them decide if it is worth their time. If a reader is confused by the headings and cannot figure out what will be said in each section, they will have no desire to read that section.

However, if they see even one or two headers that specifically pique their interest, they will be more likely to read on. Readers will be turned off by sloppy captions as well, whereas well-written captions will help them engage further with the content from the start.

Additionally, readers can become overwhelmed by overly detailed indexes or disengaged with overly brief indexes. Although these elements seem small, they serve as the signposts that allow the writer to communicate the purpose of the text, summarize, and highlight the key takeaways. That said, each of these elements is crucial for slowing a reader down in their tracks and drawing them into what the writer has to say. The engagement with these elements should compose at least half of the editing journey.

Tying up Loose Ends

As the editor (of your work or someone else's), it is your job to tie up loose ends and ensure the presented content is clear and well-supported. The hope of every editor of someone else's writing is that the writer will have done some of this work on their own first (for example, by reading aloud).

However, this is not always the case; as many times, the writer will have burnt out from the writing process and will feel that they cannot look at the text any longer. As the editor, you must be able to work with the content in hand, no matter what state it is in. In the cases of editors working for clients, this may look like doing the "dirty work" the writer did not have the energy to do—writing the copy for headings, captions, or any other missing elements. If you are both the writer and the editor, you must be able to enter into a new space in the editing process, in which you are prepared to take on this "dirty work" with a fresh mind.

Conducting Regular Check-ins

After you have checked for grammatical errors, punctuation errors, and spelling errors in the main text, it is good to check for the same things in things like the major headings and the names of people in the manuscript. This check-over should occur in both the manuscript and proofing stages, as errors can be missed even with several editing passes. The last thing you want to happen is to catch these errors once a piece of writing is already published, and the only way to avoid this is by being as meticulous as possible in the editing stages.

Writing Headings and Subheadings

Headings and subheadings must be consistent with pre-established formatting, and they should all look the same (same font, same size, same position, same general length). In general, these elements of all main headings such as chapter titles, 'Contents,' 'Preface,' 'Index,' and 'Appendix' should follow the same model. These headings should be organized logically, separating the text into easy-to-follow sections. Titles should usually have more space above than below them, with spacing varying slightly depending on the heading's importance (for example, a critical heading may be provided with more space, have a larger font sized, and be centered with more space than the average subheading).

Essential articles are marked by the most massive headlines, which should be placed near the top of the page to avoid imbalance. Another tip is to use short words in headings and subheadings as often as possible to avoid confusion that can arise from overusing hyphens.

Not only do headings and subheadings need to be correctly formatted and consistent with one another, but they also need to grab the reader's attention and make them want to read on. In many cases, the writing draft may have some headings in place by the time they reach the editing stage. However, just because the titles exist does not mean they are influential or will serve the purpose of drawing readers closer. Publications will be more successful if they have headers that make a clear statement, impress advertisers, and keep readers feeling hungry for more. If this job is not accomplished in the first drafts, it is the editor's job to rewrite the headers to make it so.

Writing and Editing Captions

When it comes to editing captions, you must remember that even if readers are not engaging deeply with the text's body, they will be naturally drawn to images and pieces of text set apart from the rest in caption form. Captions should be kept short and relevant and should be conclusive with what is happening in the illustration and the surrounding body text. Ideally, the reader will be able to understand what is happening on the page by merely examining a clear-cut caption. As the editor, you must be aware of any cross-references in the text which correspond to illustrations and make sure the figure numbers in the captions line up. It is best to use as few page numbers in cross-references as possible to save yourself the cost and the possibility of requiring further edits.

Dividing the Process into Stages

If you're feeling overwhelmed by the intensity of the editing process, don't worry. There are undoubtedly many things to consider, and the stakes are high for catching as many edits as possible to avoid misprints and ensure the publications' success. That said, there is an excellent technique for keeping yourself on track and preventing overwhelm in the editing stage. This technique involves splitting up each of these "smaller elements" of the writing and focusing on them one at a time. Start with the headings. Confer with your guidelines on which font style, size, and spacing to use in the titles and subheadings, and check them through for consistency. After you have gone over the headings several times, move on to captions. Once again, confer with the guidelines for caption writing.

With each caption, ask yourself if it is clear, concise, and in line with what is happening in the image and the rest of the text. After captions, move on to tables and content lists. Make sure the content lists direct readers to where they need to go to find specific information. As for the tables, make sure the information provided highlights the text's main points or provides the reader with necessary background information (like statistics of case studies).

Next, move on to the index and appendix. Check each one to ensure it contains just the right amount of detail, not too much, and not too little. By breaking up each of these steps and dedicating time to each, you are more likely to catch inconsistencies.

Chapter 4: Step 4 - Utilizing Isolation Strategies

As you move through the editing process, it may become gradually more difficult to tell one idea of the text from the next. After a while, words begin to meld together, and the overall context may become muddled. To keep a clear perspective with each text block, you need to be proactive with text isolation strategies. Later in the guide, we will explore further strategies for maintaining clarity, such as taking space from the text and reading in reverse. However, these strategies generally take place after the manuscript has undergone several editing passes. For this chapter, we will focus on methods of text isolation in the early stages of editing.

Keeping the Focus

Throughout the initial editing process, it can be helpful to use a blank sheet of paper to cover the text you have not yet reviewed. By doing this, you can keep your attention focused on the text at hand instead of looking ahead or becoming distracted. As you finish reading specific paragraphs, make a mark to show that you have looked at them, and don't go back until you are in the next full editing pass.

Breaking the Text into Sections

Another strategy of isolation goes hand-in-hand with the concept of taking space. Depending on your project's length, it is a good idea to establish how you will break up the text before beginning your editing process. It is very difficult to be thorough in the copyediting stages if you don't create small "cut off points" or benchmarks to keep you on track. If you are editing a poem of six stanzas with four lines in each stanza, it would be smart to give yourself about half an hour to work with the material.

Take about four minutes per stanza, with one minute dedicated to each line. You can use this minute to read the line aloud, isolated from all the rest of the poem, to check for flow and word choice. After you have finished all four lines of a particular stanza, take one minute to evaluate the stanza as a whole. Take a moment to breathe, then move on to the following stanza.

Considering Interest Level and Familiarity

On the other hand, if you are editing a 300-page book, the process of text isolation will look much different. You should begin by asking yourself how easy or challenging this particular content is for you to edit. Is it a topic you're familiar with, or is it entirely new knowledge that may take longer to process and could require additional research? Is it something that piques your interest, or is it out of your general interest area and could become tedious as you go along? Is the book written for young audiences and will be a quick and easy read, or is it designed to be intellectually challenging and maybe more time consuming to get through?

Knowing the answer to all of these questions ahead of time will make it much easier for you to understand how to divide the text into isolated sections. Not only will this allow you to be more thorough, but it will also make the process of editing much more manageable. Once you have determined the project's density and your interest level and familiarity, it's time to develop a system for breaking up the text.

Working Through Sections Quickly

If you are familiar with the content in the 300-page book and find it reasonably interesting, you will likely be able to work faster. In this case, you may choose to divide the 300-pages up into ten sections of ten pages, which you can read through fairly quickly. In between each area, take a brief break to look away from the text you just read, leaving it in the past as you move on to a new isolated piece of text. During this break, you may choose to be on your phone, use the restroom, or take a drink of water. Regardless of what you do, make sure to clear your head of the text you just read (besides the general context that you will need to take with you), and allow yourself to move on fully to the next piece.

Determining How Many Sections to Read Per Day

Once you've developed a general system of section-lengths and subsequent breaks, you can decide how many sections to read per day. If each section of ten pages takes fifteen minutes to read, you may choose to do the work in two days, putting in 1-2 hours of work per day. With each isolated section of the text, be sure to give yourself a few moments to reflect upon what you just read, and make notes of your questions and observations to refer back to on the following editing pass.

Working Through Dense Content

If the 300-page book is dense content that is harder for you to understand or feel interested in, you can expect that it will take more time, and you may also need longer breaks in between. You may decide, for example, to divide the readings up into ten-page sections but give yourself 30-40 minutes to complete them. After sitting down for this amount of time to edit a ten-page section, you may find yourself ready for a more extended break, like having a meal, going to exercise, going to a meeting, or merely doing another activity. You can expect this project to be more slow-going and should propose your deadlines as such.

If the sections are denser and take more time and mental energy, you should expect to get through fewer sections each day. Ultimately, it is best to take the time you need to make thorough edits of each isolated area, analyze that section, and carefully write down any notes you have instead of trying to power through the text.

Chapter 5: Step 5 - Interacting for Deeper Engagement

One of the best ways to stay engaged with the editing process is to interact with the text. Interacting with the text can take on numerous forms, from making physical marks on punctuation, grammar, and spelling, to taking a creative spin on reading the story from various character's perspectives. As the editor, it is your job to be fully engaged with the texts at all times, sometimes even more than the writer was. Passivity is a grave mistake in an editor and should be avoided at all costs.

The editor must be a reader who can avoid surface level word processing and truly gain something from the text, to offer meaningful feedback in return. In general, interacting with the text helps editors to avoid falling into passive reading and maintain high activity as they go along. This may look like using the imagination, wondering about further possibilities, asking questions, making analyses and evaluations, and otherwise thinking deeply. Through these tactics, editors will have higher levels of comprehension of what they read. Therefore, they will be able to offer more meaningful edits and suggestions to the writer (or make more meaningful edits to their own writing if they are the writer).

Benefits of Deep Text Interaction

There are several benefits to more in-depth interaction with the text in the editing stages, all of which help make the piece of writing as clear, concise, engaging, and error-free as possible. This deeper interaction helps the editor to think deeply about what they are reading and pinpoint when they feel confused or find themselves drifting off. If the editor feels confused at a certain point in the text, that's a good sign that the author needs to re-work that section of text for clarification purposes.

If the editor begins to drift off and has trouble paying attention to the words in front of them, that's a good sign that the writer should move that section of the text, add more colorful language, or remove it entirely. Text interaction helps to fill in any gaps in comprehension and urge the editor to reflect on both what they have taken from the text and what they anticipate for the future.

Physical Interaction Method

The first method of text interaction is physical interaction. This comes through editing methods, which keep the editor's brain engaged in a particular action system. An example of this would be to develop a table of individual edits to apply to punctuation, grammatical, and spelling errors. Perhaps the editor chooses to place an "x" symbol over every area of the text where there is an unnecessary comma, a circle around areas lacking punctuation, three lines under letters that are incorrectly capitalized, and short underlines under words that should be removed or changed. They may choose to underline or bracket the sentences or sections that capture their attention the most and circle the sentences or paragraphs to find themselves feeling lost or bored.

In terms of spelling, if the editor knows a word is misspelled, they may put it in a circle or box, and if they have questions about the spelling or meaning of a word, they may put a question mark. They could also use arrows to indicate where individual sentences should be moved.

Using a physical symbols system keeps the editor's brain on task while they work and helps them keep from getting lost when they try to refer back to the text. It also gives the writer something to look at so they can see all of the places in the text where the editor found issues. This physical interaction provides the editor with something to do as they read, which is enjoyable and useful for keeping the process on track.

Physical interaction is a deliberate act and can be especially helpful if the editor is working with a piece that they do not find naturally attractive or challenging them more than usual. The physical actions may make the task less daunting, and the editor will have more confidence in what they can do.

Personal Interaction Method

Another method of interaction is personal interaction. To do this, the editor may take the approach of building personal connections with the text by relating it to their own experience or understanding of the world. They may engage with the text by asking particular questions of themselves, such as: "How do I feel when I read this scene?" "What are my emotions towards this character?" "Whose side am I on/Who am I rooting for?" "What do I want the outcome of this piece of writing to be?" "Am I pleased with what just happened in this scene?" "What is confusing to me about this scene?" "What have I learned from this piece of writing?" "What new perspective have I gained?".

It's a good idea to make a list of questions such as these for the editor to answer as they go along. By building these personal connections, the editor will begin to feel like there is more at stake for themselves and their personal life. Their interest levels will be higher, and they will be more intentional and less likely to become distracted. Additionally, their answers to these questions should indicate whether or not the writer has done their job.

Every editor should approach their editing projects with the goal of reading to learn. They should comprehensively analyze the text, integrate new ideas and perceptions, and offer feedback that stems from a place of genuine interest and understanding of what the writer wants to convey.

Chapter 6: Step 6 - Letting Things Sit

Most editors have had the experience of growing bored with the piece of writing in front of them and growing exhausted from reading the same characters, dialogues, and scenes over and over again. This is called burnout, and as an editor, you can almost certainly expect it to happen to you. Editing can be a tedious process, especially once you're a few editing passes in. This is a natural and normal part of the process, but it is not productive. Once you have reached this point, the best way to get back on track is to grant yourself time to step away. Go out and live your life for a few hours, a day, or a few days, without having to think about the editing project at hand. Give yourself a chance to read, engage with other things you enjoy, relax, watch the people and things going on around you, and gain some fresh perspective.

When you come back to the editing process, you can do so with "fresh eyes" and a new perspective for the content in front of you. With this fresh perspective, you will not only enjoy the process more and feel more energized; you will also be able to catch things you did not notice before and offer new critiques. In some cases, you may even find yourself suggesting the writer bring in an entirely new idea or change the focus of individual sections entirely.

Choosing to Take a Break When Frustrated

Looking over the same piece of writing over and over can cause the work to become stale. No editor is unfamiliar with the feeling that comes when you're sitting at your desk, looking at the same project, and nothing is coming forth. Although you know you should have more to say and that there are undoubtedly more edits to make, nothing is coming to you. It is expected that you will start to feel tired throughout the editing process and have trouble focusing as you read the same section for the third or fourth time. You may find yourself beginning to feel frustrated and not know how much more you can do. You may also be dealing with a flustered writer (or, perhaps, you are this flustered writer) who just can't seem to find what "works."

Frustration is usually a good sign that it is time to take a step back. If you find yourself losing sight of the purpose of the writing and the enjoyment in the process of editing it, you will benefit the most from giving yourself a break. If you feel like you have to force yourself through every page, give yourself space from the text to think about what isn't working, get back in touch with your creativity, restore your energy, and bring back some fresh ideas.

Choosing to take a break can save you hours of staring at a screen or page and not comprehending any of the words in front of you. When you take a step back, take some time to remind yourself of the writer's (or your own) purpose in writing this piece. Ask yourself, "What's the point?" and give yourself time to meditate on that while you take a break from it. It's also important not to make yourself miserable throughout the writing process. If you start to feel yourself continuously wrapped up in negative emotions from the stress of editing, do yourself a favor and give yourself some time to rest, breathe, and do things that bring you joy.

Tuning into Your Surroundings

One method for giving your editing space while still gathering perspectives, which will be beneficial when you return, is to tune in to your surroundings when you go out. While you are taking your break from editing, pay particular attention to the people you see around you at the grocery store, in the park, at the mall, or on the streets.

Watch the way they interact with each other; note the way they use body language and the way they engage in daily dialogue. Suppose you're editing a piece of writing that involves character dialogue. In that case, you can take inspiration from the real world to see if the dialogue you're editing sounds realistic and flows well or if it sounds unnatural and hard to follow. As you listen to everyday people engage in conversation, you may realize that some of the dialogue in the piece you're editing sounds too formal or boring. The natural world is full of inspiration, and taking a break to simply inhabit the world can be revolutionary to your editing style.

Strengthening Character Development from Real-World People

This observation of everyday people can also give you more insight to offer the writer on how to develop their characters. You may have the idea of realistic descriptions to add to a particular character to make them seem more relatable, an action they can take that would surprise the reader, etc. You may even have an idea for a new character goal, or a new character entirely, which you can present to the writer (or bring into the piece yourself if you are the writer). Observing a couple in love on a park bench, the exact way they touch each other, how they move their heads to look at each other, and how they speak could form the way you reframe such a circumstance as you edit the writing.

You may see an older woman in the supermarket who reminds you of one of the characters in the piece you are editing. You can take down some brief observations to bring into her character description to become more realistic. As you discreetly observe body language and general human interactions, you may be able to provide further tips for the writer to create scenes the readers can visualize and relate to. The more the reader can visually see what is happening and establish a sense of interest and relatability with the characters, the more inclined they will be to continue reading.

You can play into this interest level by relating the characters in the work you're editing to people you see in your everyday life. If you are editing a piece of writing that involves a motorcyclist named Haven, for example, and you see a woman in a café who rides a motorcycle and reminds you of how the character of Haven may be in real life, you can draw inspiration from the way she drinks her coffee, the tattoos on her arms, etc. In this way, simple observation of real human beings can revolutionize character development and improvement in the editing stage.

Reading for Other Purposes

Another essential thing to do while taking your break from editing is to engage with other author's writing. In many cases, you cannot engage with work you are editing as you would if it were merely a book you picked up off the shelf. The content may be something that is not interesting to you, or you may simply not be able to feel interested because you have too much work to do with finding errors and making suggestions. For this reason, it is crucial always to have something you are reading for pure enjoyment and learning, rather than editing.

As you read the work of other authors you enjoy, ask yourself questions like, "What about this piece of writing captures my attention, and how does the author maintain it?" "Do I care about the characters in this story? If so, why do I care? If not, why not?" "How does the author keep this story moving forward and keep me from becoming bored?" You can improve your editing skills drastically by understanding the techniques used by the authors you like and making similar suggestions to the authors you work with (or applying them to your writing). If you or the author feel like the piece of writing needs something more but can't progress beyond where it is, you can use other writers' work to remind yourself how to bring in extra elements that maintain reader interest.

Move the Mind, Move the Body

Most writers and editors will tell you that moving the body is crucial, especially when your brain is constantly active. Sometimes, your thoughts will become so chaotic and activated that they don't know where to go, and it can become hard to continue the editing process in this state. Mental and physical activity go hand in hand, and you indeed cannot have one without the other. Exercise keeps our brains clear, our moods positive, and our emotions even, which are all critical throughout the editing process's challenges. In many cases, sitting down to edit after a workout is excellent because your mind will be crystal clear, your endorphins will be freely flowing, and you will likely feel more in control and ready to tackle your task.

Editing is a stressful process, and exercise is the perfect way to release that buildup of stress. This doesn't need to get a gym membership or join the community sand volleyball league; it merely means you need to find the way that works best for you to move your body and use it (especially during the editing process). In many cases, a nice jog, yoga practice, dance workout video, or walk around the neighborhood can be the perfect release of endorphins and a way to refocus your brain for when you come back to editing. Whatever type of exercise it takes for you to release your stress, clear your head, and revive your energy, give yourself time to step away and do it.

Giving Yourself Adequate Time

In every step of the editing process, it is important to give yourself plenty of time. If you rush your deadlines and set crunched timelines for yourself, you will not be able to be as clear-headed and thorough. Ultimately, this will result in a less refined piece of writing. While it is easy to become so caught up in the editing process that you feel desperate just to get it done, this can pose a great threat to the work's quality. Be sure not to short yourself on time. Editing is a process that cannot be rushed, and you need to allow for plenty of space to take breaks to make the most intentional edits possible. If you're wondering how long your breaks should be or how much time you should request to meet your editing deadlines, remember that the writing will ultimately benefit from any space you take away from it.

Try your best to keep guilty feelings at bay and value your own time, energy, and general enjoyment in the process. If you are editing for another writer, it is important to have a transparent conversation with them about the importance of breaks and taking space from the writing. Clarify your needs and why you are setting a particular deadline. This will help the author understand your process, which will ultimately put less pressure on you and allow you to do your absolute best.

Redirecting Energy on the "Off Days"

If you sit down to write one day and you feel overwhelmed by negative emotions, lack of motivation, or general disinterest, it's probably not a day you should be writing. In a society that is very driven towards production and meeting deadlines, it's hard to believe it would be okay to change your plans on a day you planned to edit. However, if you don't feel like this is the right day for you to do hours of editing, it probably isn't.

With good planning, you can provide this flexibility for yourself. It's okay for today not to be the right day to edit the way you planned. Instead, decide how you're going to spend the day giving yourself a break, re-cultivating your interest, and drawing interest from the world around you. Just because you're not doing the editing in your traditional process doesn't mean you can't gain experience from reading, taking notes of the things you observe in the world around you, and giving yourself time for the things you need and the things that bring you relaxation and joy. Editing is a draining process, and the more drained you become, the less quality work you will perform. If you sit down and realize today isn't the day for editing, allow yourself to step away, redirecting that energy to a place where it can be productive, then come back tomorrow.

Planning Breaks Ahead of Time

On a typical editing day, it's not a good idea to sit down for hours at a time and try to get everything done. If you do this, your brain may become desensitized to issues with style or other edits that need to be made and start automatically filling in the gaps that need your attention. If you plan to write for four hours, it's a good idea to decide how long your breaks will be within that period. Even if you take just five minutes every hour to stand up, stretch, drink some water, or step outside for a breath of air, your writing process will thank you immensely. You may also try an approach where you write for several hours a day for two days, then take a day to step away. In some cases, however, you may need even longer. Deadlines permitting, you may need to step away for several weeks or even months.

This is especially useful if you are trying to edit your writing and find yourself hitting walls. Give yourself time to live your life, and during that time, you'll be surprised at the new observations, perspective, and energy to bring back to the editing process when you're ready.

Chapter 7: Step 7 - Editing in Reverse

Let's say you have read and edited the same piece of writing several times, and you're beginning to hit a wall. You know that there is more to do, but you can't quite figure it out. You have indicated the writer's main goals, determined where the tension and crisis points are, paid attention to the momentum at various points throughout, made basic grammatical, spelling, and punctuation edits, checked for consistency and clarity, and even read the manuscript aloud. All of the standard editing boxes are checked, yet you still feel that something is missing. This is where editing in reverse comes in.

Overcoming Preconceptions, Deepening Concentration

As discussed previously, your brain automatically fills in the gaps as you edit. When it isn't necessary to focus on every word to get the text's main point, it's common to miss places where the flow is not as smooth as it should be, words are misspelled, or faulty punctuation is used. Putting things in reverse (meaning starting with the last sentence and making your way up) helps to hone your focus on each word and sentence in a new way.

Editing in reverse forces your brain to confront what feels like entirely new information. You will have to slow down and read each word and sentence as if it is the first time you've ever seen it. In many ways, it is the first time you've ever seen it because by reading in a different order, you are automatically unable to operate under the same unconscious assumptions of the plot. The more comfortable you are with the flow of the story and the plot, the more likely you'll be to miss problem areas. Reading in reverse allows you to disrupt this comfort, go against your unconscious assumptions, and genuinely engage with the text with fresh eyes.

When you start from the end, your brain can't assume that "we already know all this," and you will therefore be able to be much more thorough. Each paragraph you read will become an entity that stands alone, which allows you to be more intentional as you examine the sentence structure and words. As you read more slowly and with greater intention and challenge, you will be more deliberate in your editing. Your concentration will deepen, and you will notice the flow of each paragraph in a way you did not before.

Beginning at the End

When you begin the process of editing in reverse, you will want to start at the very end of the manuscript. You may choose to read the pages in the standard order, from top to bottom, but you can read from bottom to top if you want an even more significant editing challenge. By taking each page and paragraph out of context you have become familiar with, you will have to look at each word and phrase and ask yourself what it accomplishes. You will want to make corrections as you go, marking up the paper or making notes in the margins. If you have a new idea for a sentence structure, try it out in the margins. If you're not sure about a correction, feel free to indicate your uncertainty using parentheses or a question mark so you can refer back later on in the editing process.

As you move through the paragraphs, you may choose to choose some method of indicating that you have finished a paragraph, so you don't look at again until the next editing pass. You may highlight a section, mark it with an asterisk, or something else of the sort.

Correcting Consistency, Punctuation, Grammar, and Spelling

Editing in reverse gives you more ability to identify inconsistencies within the text. You may find, for example, that a character is present in a scene they shouldn't be in, or perhaps that a scene is placed in the wrong order. You're more likely to catch these things if you're reading the text in a different way than you're used to. Some of the other things you'll be looking for in the reverse editing stage are punctuation, spelling, and grammar errors.

Identifying Overuse

However, there are several other emphasis areas you should keep in mind, as well. The first of these is the overuse of certain words. Every writer has words they overuse, which can cause the manuscript to lose its flavor. As you read through the manuscript in reverse, highlight, or underline every time the writer uses a similar word. Perhaps they overuse the adjective "beautiful", or the phrase "That being said." After identifying the overused words and phrases, you can easily use a Google search or another simple tool to identify supplementary words and phrases the writer could use instead.

Identifying "Non" Words

Another thing to look out for in the reverse editing process is the use of "non" words. These are the words that can easily be removed without changing anything about the sentence meaning. In many cases, these words are "dead" to the sentence, meaning they make it less impactful and break the flow. There are thousands of "non" words out there, with the words "just," "really," and "very" being just a few.

Drafting in Reverse

In addition to editing in reverse, many editors also find it helpful to draft a reverse outline to check the work. The process of reversal outlining involves taking away all supporting evidence and details and leaving yourself with only the writer's main ideas. You should be able to define these main ideas using bullet-points, which you should ensure are placed in a logical order. This provides a condensed version of the piece of writing, in which the writer can confront if all of their goals have genuinely been met in their main points. After you have generated a reverse outline of the main points you gathered in the editing process, the writer will better understand the places where they need to provide more evidence, expand or condense a scene, or move things around for better organization.

Keeping Author Goals in Mind

The reverse outline cannot be created until the writer has completed a draft and provided it to you to describe their goals. Once you are aware of the goals, you can proceed through the manuscript with a sense of alertness about what is being accomplished in each chapter and paragraph. Before you begin editing, ask the author to present you with a basic outline that lists their writing's main ideas as they understand them. This outline will serve as something to refer back to throughout the editing process and give you something to question. As you begin making your reverse outline, consider using numbers with each bulleted point to keep yourself on track with which paragraph or chapter talks about what.

Answering Crucial Questions

The most critical point of a reverse outline is to answer questions. As you go through each paragraph, section, or chapter, ask yourself if they accurately relate to the author's expressed goals. This strategy will help you catch any scenes or pieces of information that seem irrelevant to the big picture and end up de-railing readers. As you proceed throughout the reverse outlining process, you may find yourself confronting new topics or ideas which are presented throughout the paper and may not relate to the main idea. In this case, the author either needs to change the main idea of the writing itself or remove the irrelevant information.

Another question you should ask yourself throughout the reverse outlining process is where the reader may have trouble feeling on track with the points' order. Are there areas where they may be confused chronologically or feel that they need more information? By asking this question, you can make editing suggestions for how the writer might rearrange the manuscript or individual paragraphs themselves to keep the reader feeling on track and tied into the writing's central theme(s).

As you examine each paragraph, make sure that you do not have any sections repeating the same idea. Although each paragraph should be relevant to the main idea, they should all say something new. If you have two paragraphs saying almost the same thing, it will help combine them, remove one, or revise so that they are each making a different point.

Editing the Specifics of Each Paragraph

It is also essential to make sure that each paragraph stays focused on a single topic. The writer should not try to cover too much ground in a single section; if they do, the reader will more easily get lost. If you identify paragraphs which try to tackle too many things, suggest that the writer separate those ideas to form further paragraphs, or cut the information out if it is not entirely relevant. Lastly, check each section for length requirements. Are they too long or too short? An excellent way to gauge this is by looking at the total number of pages. The longer the piece of writing, the less of a problem it is to have a few longer paragraphs. That said, it is vital to check each paragraph in-depth to make sure that it fits with the flow of the rest of the piece.

Conclusion

When you started this guide, you likely approached it as either the editor of another writer's work or with the desire to edit your writing thoroughly. You picked up this guide with the understanding that in-depth editing is crucial to the overall success of the piece that is being written and that errors in structure, clarity, punctuation, grammar, dialogue, and flow can have a drastically negative impact on how others receive your writing. You were likely aware of all that is at stake in the editing process, especially when it comes to maintaining the interest, understanding, and general respect of readers.

No matter how incredible a story's content is, too many spelling errors, grammatical mistakes, or inconsistencies can ruin the whole experience for a reader. When it comes to the editing stage, you must come prepared for the fact that how thorough you edit the book can make or break the levels of respect, and subsequent sales, it will have. When you edit your work, you should do so not only to create work you can be truly proud of, but also to cultivate a community of followers who have a deep respect for the work you produce.

Throughout the guide, you were provided with the ins and outs of the editing process, from the structural, line editing, and copywriting stages, to the importance of reading aloud, to the seemingly minor details of formatting, to deeply engaging with the content to a point where you can ensure reader impact. You became aware of the risks of missing small pieces if you become careless, and you learned how to be more thorough when it comes to catching these small pieces before it's too late.

You were provided with tips for keeping yourself engaged and present with the work you do. You also learned the benefits of creating a network of friends, followers, trusted writers, and perhaps other editors into your editing process for extra support and perspective. You learned how to maintain a fresh perspective while honoring your own energy by taking breaks, giving the writing space to breathe, taking inspiration from your surroundings, editing in reverse, and creating reverse outlines to clarify the author's main points.

You discovered the importance of being thorough and conducting as many editing passes as necessary to get the writing as close to perfect as possible. You were shown the benefits of reading work aloud to yourself and other people, because hearing it in your own voice can bring attention to details that are easy to skip while reading. You learned how to isolate parts of the text to scan for clarity and cohesivity, as well as how to step outside the original context of the text to slow down and hone in on the smaller details. Additionally, you came to understand some of the best editors' secrets and how to monitor your text for efficiency and full reader engagement.

At the end of the guide, you were provided with fresh ways to work with the text at hand to keep yourself alert and conscious of changes that still need to be made. This will help you save from being burnt out and becoming careless with your editing process. The better job you do as an editor, the more the reader will enjoy their engagement with it, and the more they will search for future pieces by you (or the writer you are editing for) in the future. No matter where you are on your editing journey, this guide is guaranteed to serve as the tool you need to keep yourself on track!

More by Jaiden Pemton

Discover all books from the Creative Writing Series by Jaiden Pemton at:

bit.ly/jaiden-pemton

Book 1: *How to Write Fiction*

Book 2: *How to Tell a Story*

Book 3: *How to Write a Screenplay*

Book 4: *How to Write Sales Copy*

Book 5: *How to Edit Writing*

Book 6: *How to Self-Publish*

Book 7: *How to Write Non-Fiction*

Book 8: *How to Write Content*

Themed book bundles available at discounted prices:

bit.ly/jaiden-pemton